MIND, BRAIN AND BEHAVIOUR:
Discussions of B. F. Skinner and J. R. Searle

MIND, BRAIN AND BEHAVIOUR:

Discussions of B.F.Skinner

and J.R.Searle

İLHAM DILMAN

ROUTLEDGE
London and New York

First published in 1988 by
Routledge
a division of Routledge, Chapman and Hall
11 New Fetter Lane, London EC4P 4EE

Published in the USA by
Routledge
a division of Routledge, Chapman and Hall, Inc.
29 West 35th Street, New York NY 10001

Printed in Great Britain
Typeset by Pat and Anne Murphy, Highcliffe-on-Sea, Dorset

British Library Cataloguing in Publication Data

Dilman, İlham
   Mind, brain and behaviour: discussions of
   B. F. Skinner and J. R. Searle
   1. Human behaviour
   I. Title
   150'.1   BF121
ISBN 0-415-00006-8

Library of Congress Cataloging-in-Publication Data
ISBN 0-415-00006-8

Contents

Preface

Behaviourism was born in the United States at the turn of the century, as a protest movement more than anything else. It grew in reaction to the idea of psychology as a science of consciousness, investigated by introspection. It redefined psychology as a study of behaviour, and ignored 'mental life' as unworthy or incapable of scientific study, or even as a fiction invented by philosophy and religion.

This conception of the subject matter of psychology, however, is one that is wedded to the philosophical presuppositions of introspectionist psychology common to Cartesian dualism. So the idea that psychology is not the study of mental life but of behaviour perpetuates the Cartesian dichotomy between mind and body — the myth that we can think of each independently of the other. The concept of consciousness it rejects is thus built on a radical divorce between mind and behaviour, for behaviourism cannot think of consciousness in any other way. Unable to find an alternative to the introspectionist account of 'mental phenomena', it reads that account into our everyday language of psychology and brands its concepts as 'mentalistic'. Consequently, it faults our language and sets itself the task of reforming it. But in doing so it inevitably changes the reality to which that language refers, and so alters the psychologist's conception and, consequently, perception of human beings. Thus where Hamlet saw man as 'like a god', Pavlov and Skinner see him as 'like a dog'.

I am talking about behaviourism as a school of psychology; that is not always the same as behaviourism as a philosophy of mind. For as a school of psychology it is concerned with developing a conceptual framework for the study of man and animals; they are the object of its study. The philosophical behaviourist, however, is concerned only with the language of psychology, with the rich variety of concepts in terms of which we raise and discuss psychological questions, such concepts as motive, intention, emotion, thought, and such distinctions as we make between voluntary and involuntary movements and actions. These are the object of its study, which is inevitably reflective.

He is concerned with understanding these concepts, not changing them. They raise certain difficulties for him which challenge his understanding. His analyses aim at surmounting these difficulties. Their success in doing so is the touchstone of their adequacy for him. But unless these analyses do justice to the actual use of the terms for these concepts in our language, we cannot consider them to be acceptable.

The behaviourist in psychology, on the other hand, is not concerned with this language primarily, but with what it is used to talk about, namely human conduct and, perhaps, animal behaviour. But the question is: How is he concerned with it? What sort of understanding does he seek? Here we have different conceptions of psychology, and that means different conceptions of man and the study of his conduct. Psychologists differ on these among themselves, hence the different schools of psychology. Here philosophy can make a contribution at two different levels: (1) It can shed light on the nature of the conflict between the different conceptions in question. (2) It can make explicit the conception we do actually take of people and their conduct 'in the traffic of human life' and ask, given the way we understand human conduct and the way that understanding enters into our very behaviour, what is its proper study?

It is true that psychology can play a role in changing our conception of man and human conduct. In his book, *Images of Man in Psychological Research* (1975), John Shotter argues that this is its main contribution to our understanding of man: 'to change our image of ourselves'. But to what purpose? No doubt it does play such a role. But in my view it does so much of the time without any clear understanding of what it is doing, guided not so much by clear ideals as goaded by confusion. In this it both makes some contribution to shaping the ethos of an age, not on its own, of course, and largely uncritically, and also reflects that ethos. This has certainly been true of behaviourism as a school of psychology. I hope to bring this out in the case of B. F. Skinner.

So what is it that behaviourism rejects in psychology? And what does it put in its place?

First, it rejects *consciousness*, sometimes describing it as a fiction, and sometimes saying that it is incapable of objective study. Here the behaviourist oscillates between wanting to reject what he calls 'mentalistic concepts' and merely dismissing an inadequate analysis of them. The trouble is that he is not altogether able to disentangle the two, so that the reductionist analyses he offers more or less amount to replacing one set of concepts with another.

Second, it rejects *introspection* as a method of investigation in psychology, the way it was used by the introspectionist school. The behaviourist is right — this was a dead end in psychology. The very idea of introspection as a species of observation is shot through with confusion, as Wittgenstein has shown conclusively. But this is not to say that our everyday idea of introspection is confused; not at all. Normally by 'introspection' we refer to a form of reflection which has oneself as its object, one's actions and conduct, one's motives, one's feelings, and one engages in it on special occasions and with specific questions in mind that trouble one. I say 'on special occasions', for generally one answers questions like 'What are your intentions?', 'What do you feel?', 'What do you think you are up to?', which others may ask one, without reflection. Normally one does not need to reflect in answering such questions, nor does what one says have a basis which one scrutinises.

The behaviourist is right to reject the idea of introspection as a species of observation — self-observation. With it, however, he rejects something important, namely the difference between the subject's and the observer's point of view, between the subject's way of answering questions about himself and a third person's way of answering these same questions about him. In his paper, 'Behaviourism as a Philosophy of Psychology' (1964), Professor Norman Malcolm sees this as the central weakness of behaviourism.

Third, behaviourism also rejects the idea of *purpose* and other connected notions such as thought, reasons, understanding, aims and intentions, as needed for understanding human conduct. It replaces these with a mechanistic scheme of which the conditioned reflex was a cornerstone in early behaviourism. Here the behaviouristic psychologist sees himself as killing two birds with one stone. For what he attempts to do is at once to purge psychological language of all 'subjective terms' and psychology of all teleology. In this way he supposes psychology will become an *objective* discipline like the physical sciences. Indeed, the claim that 'mind is an illusion' incorporates these two ideas: (a) mind is nothing over and above behaviour — what psychologists call 'cognitive states' are myths or fictions, and (b) all human and animal actions alike are mechanically or causally determined.

Descartes had held the opposite of both views, namely (a) that mind is consciousness and thought, and (b) that as such it is the source of all intelligent or intentional action, including speech. Men are capable of such actions, whereas beasts are not. Behaviourist philosophers have generally been concerned with rejecting the former of these two Cartesian claims because, in the way it was conceived by Descartes, it leads to solipsism. The behaviourist school of psychology, on the other hand, has been opposed to both of these claims. Its view is not merely that beasts are not capable of intentional action, but that men are not capable of it either, the notions of intentional action and human agency being regarded as parts of a mythology. In this behaviouristic thinking is the heir of Thomas Hobbes' conception of man.

Indeed, the attempt to reject teleology and purge our concept of behaviour from the shadow which purpose casts on it has far-reaching consequences. You cannot do so without radically altering our concept of behaviour. Thus behaviourism is committed, not only to a reductionist analysis of mind and all mental concepts ('mind is nothing over and above behaviour'), but also to a reductionist analysis of behaviour, the whole of human conduct and actions ('behaviour is nothing over and above reflex movements'). Further, its stimulus–response approach to behaviour fails to recognise the distinction between what is voluntary and what is not, and between reason and cause — 'cause' in the sense it is used in the applied sciences. It is atomistic, not only in its conception of actions as made up of and so analysable into movements or atomic responses. It is also atomistic in its conception of man's behavioural environment as made up of and so analysable into stimuli. Both these conceptions have been criticised by Gestalt psychologists.

Skinner has been the most influential of behaviourists in psychology. In my discussion of him my aim is to highlight the main features of his thinking, expose where he has gone wrong and the philosophical presuppositions responsible for his errors. It is important to see that it *has* gone wrong, badly wrong, and exactly where and how. To expose these defects, to appreciate the way they are tied together, is a matter of philosophical criticism, and it does not constitute an intrusion of an alien discipline into psychology — as if, *a priori*, armchair considerations were being thrust in the way of an empirical inquiry and made to obstruct its progress.

Anybody who is capable of thinking on the questions to which Skinner believes to have made a radically new contribution has a right to question the appropriateness of his methods and to challenge its pretensions. When I say 'thinking on these questions' I am not referring to philosophy, but to the knowledge or capacity presupposed in doing philosophical psychology, a capacity we all share. Skinner, therefore, does not have a privileged knowledge or understanding of these questions and the concept of human life of which they form a part. The question of the appropriateness of his methodology is not itself an empirical question. Besides the analysis of psychological concepts on which Skinner's methodology rests is a philosophical analysis and so is answerable to philosophical criticism. As for Skinner's hopes and pretensions, they are clearly extra-scientific, and their very *naiveté* stands out for anyone who can distance himself from the headiness of Skinner's enterprise, detach himself from its presuppositions, which go deep in academic psychology, and remind himself of the kind of understanding we seek in human affairs.

There is nothing dualistic about that understanding. The thought that it is dualistic and pre-scientific is the result of Skinner's own philosophical confusion.

So much for my defence of a philosophical critique of Skinner's thought. Perhaps I should add that the hopes and aspirations that belong with a methodology like Skinner's are expressions of an ethos that shapes the consciousness of an age — one which finds expression in other walks of life and phenomena of culture, including contemporary movements in philosophy. Insofar as a philosopher is drawn into such a movement he could, if he were influential, himself play a part, however small, in the shaping of contemporary consciousness. It is important, therefore, that he should stand out and not be an uncritical party to it. For this he needs to have a wider base of sustenance in the history of philosophy and the traditions that form part of that history.

To return to Skinner. Even if his particular influence is waning, the type of thinking he represents is still dominant in mainstream psychology. Therefore a critical discussion of his conception of man, the kind of life of which he is capable, and the study of his conduct, as well as of Skinner's view of what is desirable for humanity, remains relevant to contemporary psychology. But in any case, the approach he represents in his study of man and its underlying presuppositions are of more long-standing philosophical interest.

In the way he represents man as an object of manipulation, in his conception of 'behavioural engineering', and in the character of the hopes he pins on it, I find Skinner reminiscent of the early Greek sophist Gorgias. I have in mind Gorgias's conception of 'oratory', its power and benefits. It is in similar ways that their conceptions of language and of human conduct respectively are defective. Gorgias described the aim of oratory as the manipulation of man's beliefs without enlightenment. Similarly, 'behavioural engineering' is the application of techniques of operant conditioning to human beings to shape their behaviour without engaging their understanding. Gorgias is sceptical about the very possibility of the enlightenment he regards as irrelevant to his teaching, the kind of knowledge or understanding apart from which language itself makes no sense. Skinner is similarly sceptical about the possibility of the kind of understanding human beings exercise as agents — hence my description of Skinner as a 'modern Gorgias'.

Of course, the understanding to which Skinner gives no room in his study of human conduct, the understanding which human beings exercise in what they do and in the way they respond to what faces them in particular situations, is constitutive of human actions and reactions. Indeed, it is constitutive of human beings as persons. Leave it out and you are no longer studying human behaviour. Behaviourism, therefore, at least Skinner's behaviourism, is not what it claims to be, namely a study of human behaviour. The picture that emerges of different aspects of it in the chapters of *Science and Human Behaviour* (1953) on 'Emotion', 'Self-control', 'Thinking', 'The Self' and so on is a grotesque caricature of these things.

I bring this out largely by letting Skinner speak for himself, on human action, intention, decision, motivation, speech and self-control. You do not have to dig to find out what is wrong with Skinner's thought. Its inadequacies are apparent. Nevertheless, they need to be underlined. For those who are steeped in the methodologies of experimental psychology do not have a clear view of them. In that sense much of what I say about Skinner's work may be obvious to everyone except those who are caught up in a way of thinking that is wider than behaviourism.

In the case of Searle this is not true. For Searle wishes to preserve our everyday conception of ourselves and, unlike Skinner, he believes that science cannot reject or modify it radically. Having said this, however, he still says some strange things about man's intentional agency and the relation of thought to action. In bringing this out, my final court of appeal is 'what everyone admits' (Wittgenstein 1963, sec. 599).

Searle's aim in his Reith lectures is to reconcile scientific materialism with our 'common-sense picture of ourselves' and to criticise materialistic theories of mind which do not respect this picture. But as a materialist himself and a builder of theories he belongs to the ethos which has produced the theories of mind which he criticises. He holds philosophy to contribute to knowledge, alongside the sciences, by large-scale intellectual constructions, and he shares Skinner's view (and for that matter Quine's and that of many other contemporary intellectuals) that all human knowledge centres round the sciences.

> Some of the greatest intellectual efforts of the twentieth century have been attempts . . . to get a science of human behaviour which was not just common sense . . . psychology, but was not scientific neurophysiology either. Up to the present time, without exception, . . . [these] efforts have been failures. Behaviourism was the most spectacular failure, but in my lifetime I have lived through exaggerated claims made on behalf of and eventually disappointed by games theory, cybernetics, information theory, structualism, sociobiology, and a bunch of others. (*Minds, Brains and Science*, 1984, p. 42)

So Searle differs from these different forms of materialism in wanting to preserve the 'common-sense psychology' which Skinner ridicules as 'animistic', 'dualistic' and 'unscientific'. He defends the mind's special status and argues that a psychology which accepts this is not, for this reason, unscientific.

His theoretical position, therefore, is a form of dualism, though Searle himself rejects such a classification as 'outmoded'. It is a dualism in the sense that when Professor Gilbert Ryle was once asked whether he was a dualist he answered, 'Yes, there are both chaps and things.' Jean-Paul Sartre too is a dualist in this sense in that he distinguishes between 'two modes of existence', one of which is that of human beings. In other words, he held that the human mode of existence is radically different from that of things. Descartes would go along with this, but he misrepresented what is distinctive about human existence by dividing the mind from the body and trying to make sense of it in separation from the kind of life human beings live with language as flesh-and-blood beings. It is well known that both Ryle and Sartre criticised what has come to be known as 'Cartesian dualism'.

Searle's dualism, on the other hand, is Cartesian. For despite the logical sophistication of his accounts of intentionality and human action, he is wedded to the presuppositions of Cartesian dualism. In this he is like most modern theorists of the mind, be it Skinner or Armstrong. But though he is a dualist in expounding a scientific view of human beings which tries to leave room for our 'common-sense picture of ourselves as human beings', ultimately he fails to do so. His theory comes to grief over the question of whether or not we possess free will and are capable of free action.

Searle does not himself recognise this. For he does not connect his failure to reconcile the causal determinism of his scientific materialism with our common-sense view of ourselves as free agents with his particular 'solution' of the mind–body problem. Ultimately, it is his materialism as an all-embracing metaphysical position that is to blame for this. What is needed here is a sense of proportion about the logical place of science in human knowledge. But that is something towards which one has to work philosophically.

In contrast with Searle, I see the task of philosophy as consisting of criticism and clarification. Accordingly, this book is a criticism of two influential theories of mind. Such criticism involves discussions of the relation between the human mind and behaviour, between the mind and the body, and in particular between thinking and the brain. This is a matter of clarifying a whole network of conceptual relations rather than constructing a model for a single wholesale relationship.

The two books by Skinner to which I refer most frequently are *Science and Human Behaviour* and *Beyond Freedom and Dignity*. When giving page references to these in the text I use the following abbreviations: *SHB* and *BFD*. The only text by Searle to which I refer is *Minds, Brains and Science*, his Reith Lectures in 1984. I therefore give page references to it without citing the title. All the books to which I refer are listed in the Bibliography. I refer to these by giving the name of the author and the date of the edition listed in the Bibliography.

İlham Dilman
September 1987

I
B. F. Skinner: a Modern Gorgias

1

Operant Conditioning

Hamlet said of man, 'How like a god!' (Act II, Scene ii). Pavlov said of him, 'How like a dog!' Skinner says. 'That was a step forward. For like a dog, man is within the range of a scientific analysis.'

With such an analysis, Skinner brought down man to a level that is little different from that at which a dog lives. He could take no account of the role which reason and considerations, interest, affection and friendship, guilt and compassion, shame and bravery, ideals and values play in human life. We shall see that for him, all the good things of life are positive reinforcers, and that calling something good is like saying 'good boy' to a dog; that for Skinner all human motivation reduces to the stereotype of the carrot and the stick.

To appreciate this we have to start with 'operant conditioning', which is the cornerstone of his thinking.

Darwin had posited the continuity of species. This was at first resisted. When it came to be accepted it was widely represented as the discovery that man is not *essentially* different from animals. Hence the use of the term 'organism' in psychology to refer to man and animals without distinction. This is the anti-Cartesian position. For on Descartes' view, while all animal behaviour and a good deal of human behaviour can be explained mechanically, speech and intelligent behaviour cannot. These are the sole property of human beings. They have their source in thinking or consciousness, and thought is the essence of the mind or soul. Human beings possess a mind or soul, and this makes them *essentially* different from animals.

But this little word 'essentially' is a tricky word. It polarises positions whose central insights need not exclude one another. In his book, *Science and Human Behaviour*, Skinner writes:

Darwin, in insisting upon the continuity of species, had questioned the belief that man was unique among the animals in his ability to think. Anecdotes in which lower animals seemed to show the 'power of reasoning' were published in great numbers. But when terms which had formerly been applied only to human behaviour were thus extended, certain questions arose concerning their meaning. Did the observed facts point to mental processes, or could these apparent evidences of thinking be explained in other ways? Eventually it became clear that the assumption of inner thought-processes was not required. Many years were to pass before the same question was seriously raised concerning human behaviour, but Thorndike's experiments and his alternative explanation of reasoning in animals were important steps in that direction. (pp. 59–60)

Köhler criticises Thorndike; Skinner ignores this criticism and builds on Thorndike's experiments. He points out that what is involved here is different from Pavlov's experiments involving the conditioned reflex. If we say that Pavlov's dog learns to salivate at the sound of a gong, what we mean is that where previously the dog did not salivate on hearing a gong, now it does. Of course, the dog does not learn to do anything, it merely acquires a new response. Obviously this is at best 'learning' in a minimal sense of the term. Skinner describes the kind of conditioning involved here as a process of stimulus substitution. The response (salivation) that was evoked by one stimulus (the sight of food) comes to be evoked by a new stimulus (the sound of a gong). The originally neutral stimulus acquires this power by being presented together or paired with the stimulus which already has it (food). The more frequently the gong is paired with the food, the stronger is the dog's conditioned response at the sound of the gong. The food is thus said to *reinforce* the conditioned response. Here it is the pairing of the reinforcer (food) with the originally neutral stimulus (the sound of the gong) which brings about the conditioning.

It is otherwise in the case of Thorndike's cat. There certain responses are 'stamped in' because they have certain *consequences* — the cat is freed from its confinement and gets food. It is this fact that reinforces the response in question. Skinner names this 'operant conditioning' in distinction from Pavlovian conditioning, which he calls 'respondent conditioning'. In Pavlovian or respondent conditioning, a conditioned response is reinforced by something that *precedes* the response reinforced; in Skinnerian or operant conditioning it is reinforced by what follows it. Nevertheless, Skinner's account of what happens here is causal and not teleological — that is, it is not in terms of final causes. Just as Pavlov wanted to eschew saying that the dog salivates on hearing the gong because it 'reminds' him of food, similarly Skinner wants to eschew saying that the cat makes the particular movement which lifts the latch and releases the door because it 'expects' that movement will lead to its getting food. His reason for wanting to eschew this is twofold: (1) Because he thinks of expectation as an inner state, and he wants to avoid any reference to inner states in the explanation of behaviour. (2) Because an expectation is directed to the future and what lies in the future cannot be a cause of what comes before it. The fact that operant behaviour seems to be 'directed towards the future [he says] is misleading' (*SHB*, p. 88). I shall return to this point.

Actually, Skinner illustrates operant conditioning with an even simpler experiment he has himself designed. Here is his own brief account of it:

> We select a relatively simple bit of behaviour which may be freely and rapidly repeated, and which is easily observed and recorded. If our experimental subject is a pigeon, for example, the behaviour of raising the head above a given height is convenient. This may be observed by sighting across the pigeon's head at a scale pinned on the far wall of the box. We first study the height at which the head is normally held and select some line on the scale which is reached only infrequently. Keeping our eye on the scale we then begin to open the food tray very quickly whenever the head rises above the line. If the experiment is conducted according to specifications the result is invariable: we observe an immediate change in the frequency with which the head crosses the line. We also observe, and this is of some importance theoretically, that higher lines are now being crossed. We may advance almost immediately to a higher line in determining when the food is to be presented. In a minute or two, the bird's posture is changed so that the top of the head seldom falls below the line which we first chose. (*SHB*, pp. 63–4)

5

In Pavlov's experiments there is no difficulty in saying that originally the sight of the food and, after the conditioning, the sound of the gong *cause* the dog to salivate. But in Skinner's experiment the food is what the pigeon *will* obtain *if* it raises its head above a certain height. Until it does so, the food is not in sight. If we say that the food is what causes the pigeon to raise its head, we are making what is not yet, what is in the future, the cause of something in the present, which is nonsense. If we say that it is the thought or expectation of food that is the cause, then we are either referring to what Skinner calls an 'inner cause' or a 'psychic cause', or our explanation is in terms of a 'final cause', that is in terms of something which the pigeon seeks to obtain or aims at obtaining. And Skinner wants to eschew both.

So he makes the following conceptual manoeuvre. The food comes after the response, raising the head or stretching the neck, and so cannot be its cause. However, if you do not make the single response the unit of your account but instead observe a whole series of responses over a certain stretch of time, then you can say that the change in the frequency of these responses (the change in the frequency with which the pigeon's head is raised above a certain mark) *is caused by* the food which the pigeon has received each time it 'emitted' (Skinner's own word) the response in question. The unit of operant conditioning is thus not an individual response, but the *probability of it*, measured in terms of the frequency of its repetition in a series over a certain period.

Skinner points out, quite rightly, that here we cannot talk of trial-and-error learning, as in Thorndike's experiment. The pigeon is not 'trying' anything. Nor is any movement which does not achieve a specified consequence an error. Even the term 'learning' is misleading. The bird does not 'learn' that it will get food by stretching its neck. Skinner doesn't want to speak of its having acquired the 'habit' of stretching its neck either, because, he says, if we were to say, 'The pigeon stretches its neck because it has acquired the habit of doing so,' this would be circular. Nor does he find the term 'response' wholly appropriate, though he finds it convenient and so keeps it. It is not wholly appropriate because there is not anything to which the raising of the head or stretching of the neck is a response, as when a human being or animal responds to a light, say, by blinking. He calls it 'operant response' to emphasise that the behaviour operates on the environment to generate consequences. In this case the consequences are artificially produced by the experimenter. But there are many cases where they are not produced artificially. For instance, smiling (Skinner's example) generates friendliness in others, which reinforces smiling at people. Or playing a piece of music on the piano the way it sounds best to the player reinforces that particular way of playing it. Thus Skinner writes:

> The consequences of behaviour may 'feed back' into the organism. When they do so, they may change the probability that the behaviour which produced them will occur again. The English language contains many words, such as 'reward' and 'punishment', which refer to this effect, but we can get a clear picture of it only through experimental analysis. (ibid., p. 59)

With regard to this feedback, Skinner says, 'The organism must be stimulated by the consequences of its behaviour if [operant] conditioning is to take place.' Where there is feedback the consequences may be 'reinforcing' or 'aversive'. In the latter case Skinner speaks of punishment. He divides reinforcers into positive and negative ones. A positive reinforcer is a consequence which reinforces the behaviour that produced it — such as food in the case of Thorndike's cat. A negative reinforcer is a consequence which removes an aversive condition — such as freedom from confinement which results from the door of Thorndike's cage coming open. Punishment, on the other hand, is the presentation of a negative reinforcer or the removal of a positive one.

In this analysis of the relation between consequences and operant responses, Skinner avoids any reference to pleasure and pain, likes and dislikes. He asks why certain consequences are reinforcing, why it is that those consequences that reinforce a certain response do so. He is well aware of the difficulties raised by Thorndike's law of effect which says that those responses which lead to success are stamped in (i.e. reinforced). What counts as success? And why should success reinforce those responses that lead to it? He says that if one were to say that an animal repeats a response when it finds the consequences 'pleasant' or 'satisfying', then either one is using 'subjective' terms which have no place in a scientific psychology, or one is referring to the effect of the consequences on the animal, in which case what one says is circular. For all that it amounts to is that 'reinforcement reinforces because it is reinforcing'. Skinner's answer is Darwinian:

> We can scarcely overlook the great biological significance of

the primary reinforcers. Food, water, and sexual contact, as well as escape from injurious conditions, are obviously connected with the well-being of the organism. An individual who is readily reinforced by such events will acquire highly efficient behaviour. It is also biologically advantageous if the behaviour due to a given reinforcement is especially likely to occur in an appropriate state of deprivation. Thus it is important, not only that any behaviour which leads to the receipt of food should become an important part of a repertoire, but that this behaviour should be particularly strong when the organism is hungry. The two advantages are presumably responsible for the fact that an organism can be reinforced in specific ways and that the result will be observed in relevant conditions of deprivation. (*SHB*, p. 83)

In *Beyond Freedom and Dignity* he says, 'All reinforcers eventually [ultimately] derive their power from evolutionary selection' (p. 104).

Thus Skinner's conception of operant conditioning is 'biologistic', in contrast with Pavlonian conditioning, which is a 'mechanistic' conception.

Pavlov and Bechterev (independently) discovered the conditioned reflex. Watson, the founder of behaviourism, had reacted to a dualistic conception of psychology and made the conditioned reflex and its S – R framework the basis of his psychology. To him, the whole of human behaviour is built up by conditioning from a relatively small number of unconditioned reflexes which he called 'squirmings'. Whether or not Skinner can be said to have discovered a different type of conditioning, he is certainly responsible for formulating the conception of 'operant conditioning' and analysing it. In my estimation this is the sum total of Skinner's contribution to psychology.

Of course, both he and his followers have a grossly inflated view of the importance of this discovery. Pavlovian conditioning (Skinner says) is concerned with reflexes, and reflexes relate to the internal physiology of the organism — e.g. salivation, pupil contraction and dilation etc. Operant conditioning, on the other hand, relates to behaviour which has some effect on the surrounding world. Pavlovian conditioning adds new controlling stimuli — salivation which was produced by the sight of food is now also produced by the dinner gong. But it does not add new responses to the individual's repertoire. Whereas operant conditioning does just that, it shapes and maintains behaviour. What we have here is a shaping of responses by their consequences. Skinner holds that all behaviour — animal and human, individual and social — is shaped and maintained in this way, and so can be controlled by operant conditioning. He holds that *all* behaviour can be understood in terms of the concepts of operant conditioning. He maintains that the modes of behaviour and interaction characteristic of different dimensions of human life (language and the way it is learned, personal interaction, moral actions and the acquiring of ethical values, art, literature, entertainment, politics, education and interest in learning) are all cases of behaviour which differ merely in *complexity* from those cases he has studied experimentally. He writes:

> Operant conditioning shapes behaviour as a sculptor shapes a lump of clay. Although at some point the sculptor seems to have produced an entirely novel object, we can always follow the process back to the original undifferentiated lump, and we can make the successive stages by which we return to this condition as small as we wish. At no point does anything emerge which is very different from what preceded it . . . The pigeon experiment demonstrates this clearly. (p. 91)

I do not see how.

Skinner goes on to claim that what the child learns in becoming an adult — to raise himself, to stand, to walk, to grasp objects and move them about, later to talk, to sing, to dance, to play games — he learns in the same way as the pigeon learns to stretch its neck higher and higher, that is 'through the reinforcement of slightly exceptional instances of his behaviour'. The child's behaviour is 'continuously modified from a basic material which is largely undifferentiated'. The later behaviour, for instance talking or playing the piano, can be broken into units whose transformation into their present form can be traced back to their earliest instances — a transformation through operant conditioning (p. 93).

So Skinner claims. But I have yet to see this claim substantiated in a particular example. I have not come across any such example in his book. All it contains are extravagant claims, never substantiated, and general analyses that are unacceptable on *a priori* grounds. It is these analyses that I intend to criticise.

9

2

Skinner's View of the Language of Psychology

Skinner's conception of everyday language in general and of psychological concepts in particular, together with his conception of psychology as a science, lead him to rewrite practically the whole of our psychological language.

He thinks of the language in which we speak about ourselves and others, and discuss human conduct, as dualistic. To Skinner this means that it incorporates a philosophy that is pre-scientific. In the name of science, then, and in the pursuit of his scientific programme for psychology, he carries out a surgery on language. What he achieves, as we shall see, is to castrate the language of psychology and to impoverish the understanding we can find through it.

Skinner is wrong to think of our everyday language of psychology as essentially dualistic. I would argue that it is itself neutral between rival philosophies of mind. Wittgenstein spoke of language as one of the prominent sources of philosophical problems. He meant that the problems come from 'misunderstandings of the logic of our language' and that these misunderstandings are themselves prompted or encouraged by the forms of our language. Notice that what is in question are misunderstandings. If we are misled by the language we speak, this is not because there is anything defective in our language. Therefore to remove those misunderstandings is not to alter our language. Philosophical theories about the nature of mind, such as Cartesian dualism, involve a certain 'reading' of psychological language. But even when that reading seeps into everyday consciousness or thought, it should not be confused with the ordinary sense of that language, with the meanings of its words. One can, therefore, combat and reject that reading without touching those meanings.

To confuse a particular reading of psychological language, such as dualism, with the meanings of its words is to share in that reading. It is to fail to make any sense of that language that is not dualistic. Because Skinner is committed to a dualistic reading of our everyday language of psychology (committed through a misunderstanding of its logic), he feels compelled to reform it. He rationalises this by drawing an analogy between what he is doing and the way innovators in the physical sciences, finding the concepts of our everyday language inadequate for their particular purposes, developed new concepts, thus distancing the language of physics from the everyday language of physical objects.

The two cases, however, are not parallel. I have two reasons for saying this. The first one is this. If the scientists Skinner has in mind found everyday language inadequate, it was so for their special purposes. There was no suggestion that the language in which we talk about physical objects is inadequate in itself, or inadequate to our purposes. On the contrary, they continued to use that language. They would have admitted that the language of physics remains related to our everyday language. Skinner, on the other hand, is all het up about our everyday language of psychology, and characterises it as 'pre-scientific' and 'animistic'. He wishes us to drop most of its locutions, to purge our thoughts of its alleged animism and anthropomorphism.

In *Beyond Freedom and Dignity* he writes as follows:

> Man's first experience with causes probably came from his own behaviour: things moved because he moved them. If other things moved, it was because someone else was moving them, and if the mover could not be seen, it was because he was invisible. The Greek gods served this way as the causes of physical phenomena. They were usually outside the things they moved, but they might enter into and 'possess' them. Physics and biology soon abandoned explanations of this sort and turned to more useful kinds of causes, but the step has not been decisively taken in the field of human behaviour. Intelligent people no longer believe that men are possessed by demons . . . but human behaviour is still commonly attributed to indwelling agents (p. 13)

He continues:

> Careless references to purpose are still to be found in both

11

physics and biology, but good practice has no place for them; yet almost everyone attributes human behaviour to intentions, purposes, aims, and goals. (p. 14)

This means, Skinner claims, that 'almost everyone who is concerned with human affairs . . . continues to talk about human behaviour in this pre-scientific way' (p. 15). He adds, 'Yet there is nothing like it in modern physics or most biology, and that fact may well explain why a science and a technology of behaviour have been so long delayed' (p. 16).

The logic behind this argument is totally spurious. Animism is the attribution of human purpose to inanimate things. Skinner himself gives examples: 'Aristotle argued that a falling body accelerated because it grew more jubilant as it found itself nearer home (*BFD*, p. 14). It is from this way of thinking that modern physics has freed us. But if attributing what is human to the non-human is defective thinking, can attributing what is human to human beings be a defect? Inanimate matter is not human, and treating it as if it were is anthropomorphism; but treating human beings as human cannot be. Surely it is Skinner's 'mechanism', namely treating human beings as non-human, that is objectionable. It is the reverse of anthropomorphism and errs in just the same way, only in the opposite direction.

So Skinner is wrong to object to the language in which we talk about human beings. That language *is* different from the language in which we talk about inanimate things. But it is neither animistic nor dualistic. In fact these are two different things which Skinner confuses. Animism is the attribution of mind to inanimate things, not the attribution of mind to human beings. The latter is not animism, nor is it dualism. Dualism is the logical divorce between mind and body. In so far as Skinner cannot think of the mind except as an entity separate from the body he is a dualist, even if he rejects the mind and proposes to treat man as nothing more than a biological organism.

My second reason for suggesting that the case of Skinner is different from that of scientists who develop new concepts is connected with this difference in logic between ourselves and the phenomena studied by these scientists. For we are ourselves language users, and our being is bound up with the language in which we speak of ourselves. You cannot, therefore, treat that language lightly and insensitively, as Skinner does, if you want to understand what we are like, the kind of beings we are. If anything is at fault here, it is not that language, but the scientific programme in the name of which Skinner proposes to reform our language.

3

Skinner's Reductive Analyses: the Mind and its States

Given his understanding of the everyday language in which we talk about ourselves, and his programme for a scientific psychology, Skinner proceeds to doctor that language in the name of science. This results in the rejection of a great many concepts, or of their familiar meanings while retaining their name, and consequently of the realities which we bring into focus in terms of these concepts. This sometimes takes the form of saying of a concept that 'there is no place for it in a scientific account of behaviour', that explanations which employ it are 'fictitious', or that the concept is 'dispensable', since it is not relevant in a functional analysis of the causes of behaviour. Sometimes it takes the form of giving a reductive analysis of propositions in which the concept occurs.

What he thus rejects may be divided roughly into five categories, although these overlap: (1) the mind and its states, (2) final causes, (3) the self and the will, (4) freedom and the autonomy of the will, (5) various moral conceptions.

Given this drastic surgery, of course, what Skinner calls 'behaviour' cannot be, and is not, what we mean and understand by that term. So one could add a sixth category to the above, namely (6) actions. I shall begin by commenting on what falls under the first of the above categories, namely the mind and its states. There is more than one ambiguity here about what Skinner rejects.

1. Skinner's idea of the mind as a little man within

To begin with, for Skinner, rejecting dualism is not rejecting the conceptual divorce between mind and body, or bridging any conceptual gaps between them. It is rejecting the existence of the mind as he conceives of it. He sometimes talks of this as a belief in 'an inner agent which lacks physical dimensions' (*SHB*, p. 29). He regards this as the last ditch into which the animism of primitive people has retreated in the civilised world. People used to think that such an inner agent, modelled on themselves, was responsible for the rain and the wind. They no longer think so, but they still think of such an agent as being responsible for human actions. As Skinner puts it: 'The inner man is regarded as driving the body very much as the man at the steering wheel drives a car. The inner man wills an action, the outer executes it. The inner loses his appetite, the outer stops eating . . . The inner has the impulse which the outer obeys' (ibid.).

Is Skinner rejecting a model for the conceptual relation between the mind and the body, or is he rejecting a primitive belief? He is by no means clear about this. In a paper ('Experimental Psychology', 1947) he speaks of what he is rejecting as an out-moded explanatory hypothesis on a par with the *vis viva* or phlogiston (pp. 29–30). But other things, he says, suggest that what is at issue is not the truth of a hypothesis but the way we are to conceive of a person's relation to his actions and emotions, in his capacities as both agent and subject, answering questions about them. The basic issue for behaviourism, he writes, is not the nature of the stuff of which the world is made or whether it is made of one type of stuff or two, but rather of the dimensions of the things studied by psychology and the methods relevant to them (1964, p. 79).

2. Skinner's idea of consciousness as a state

Secondly, he speaks as if what he is rejecting is 'consciousness', 'mental states', 'inner states' or 'cognitive states'. He sometimes talks of 'intervening states' and 'mediators'. But is he rejecting what cognitive psychologists and Cartesian philosophers call 'mental states', 'cognitive processes', or such of our everyday concepts as seeing, thought, memory, expectation, intention, emotion, need and want? These are not the same thing. For it can be argued, for instance, that intentions are not mental states, that to think of them in this way is to misunderstand the logic of the term 'intention'. This is not to reject the notion of intention, to purge our discourse on human action and behaviour from all reference to the agent's intentions. It is to reject a certain analysis of 'intention' as inadequate. But Skinner is unclear about this and runs the two together. For he himself tends to think of such notions as intention in Cartesian terms. Consequently, he cannot reject Cartesian dualism, that is, the dualistic analysis of these everyday notions, without doing violence to our language.

In 'Behaviourism at Fifty' he argues as follows. Darwin established the continuity between species. This means that a human being is not essentially different from an animal. Consequently, we can resort to human terms in explaining a dog's or a cat's behaviour; for instance, we can attribute consciousness or reasoning to it; or we can move in the opposite direction and question the evidence for consciousness and reasoning in man. Lloyd Morgan questioned this in animals with his Canon of Parsimony, and Thorndike offered an alternative explanation of the supposedly intelligent behaviour of cats. But 'if evidence for consciousness and reasoning could be explained in other ways in animals, why not also in man?' His answer is to attempt to explain all human action and learning in terms of operant conditioning. This is a substantive, radical claim. In the chapters that follow I shall try to bring out how utterly and deeply confused a claim this is.

Skinner sees himself as developing the same point:

> Freud contributed to the behaviouristic argument by showing that mental activity did not, at least, *require* consciousness. His proof that thinking had occurred without introspective recognition was, indeed, clearly in the spirit of Lloyd Morgan. They were operational analyses of mental life. (p. 82)

They were nothing of the kind. Freud was not a behaviourist, nor was he in any way sympathetic to behaviourism. What he argued was that a person can think or feel something without recognising this, in other words that he can deceive himself about his own thoughts and feelings. From the fact that in this sense 'mental activity does not require consciousness' it does not follow that one can dispense with consciousness altogether, claim that human beings are not conscious beings, that is, sentient and capable of thought. Freud's proof of the unconscious is not at all in the spirit of Lloyd Morgan. With his twin concepts of the unconscious and repression, Freud was putting forward something positive he had recognised about human beings. In what he says, Skinner reads his own conclusion into Freud with a complete disregard of Freud's concerns.

So what Skinner's rejection of consciousness comes to is this. He sees himself as extending Thorndike's 'objective study of behaviour', without recourse to consciousness and reasoning, to cover the many cases of human behaviour. Having done so, however, he says that 'behaviourists do not "ignore" consciousness. On the contrary, they have developed reasonably successful ways of talking about it' ('Answer to my Critics', 1973, p. 257). But does Skinner mean that he has developed reasonably successful ways for talking about phenomena traditionally attributed to consciousness — intentional action, desire, pleasure, aversion, etc. — or that he does not deny what he calls 'private events'? If the former, I would say that his way of talking about such human phenomena is far from successful. If the latter, then what he calls 'private events' is a travesty of what one may call the inner dimension of human life. I shall comment on both points below.

Sometimes, however, when Skinner talks of rejecting consciousness and mental states, what he is doing is rejecting a cognitivist conceptual mythology. Here I am at one with him. For instance, when discussing Pavlov's discovery of the conditioned reflex and rejection of 'psychic secretion', he comments that 'there is no additional mental process in which the dog "associates the sound of the tone with the idea of food" or in which it salivates because it "expects" food to appear' (*SHB*, pp. 53–54). What he rejects here is the idea that there must be an intervening state. It could be said that the dog's expectation of food is *in* his response to the sound, that the salivation in these circumstances is an *expression* of the dog's expectation of food. In that case, what is being denied is *not* that the dog expects food, but that expectation is an inner state behind the response. But Skinner is not clear about this.

Let me give one or two other examples. The dog goes to the place where he buried a bone the previous evening and digs the bone out. We say that the dog has remembered. We are not denying this if we say that no mental process of remembering takes place. What we are denying is not that the dog has remembered, but that remembering is a mental process — such as the occurrence of mental pictures for instance. No such pictures need occur when someone remembers; but even when they do, the pictures themselves do not constitute the remembering. This conceptual point, however, has little to do with the claims of behaviourism.

Another example. I see someone; his face looks vaguely familiar. I then recognise him. What does my recognition consist of? Is it an inner state, something I can know by introspection?

No, nothing that takes place within me can amount to my recognising him apart from my remembering his name, asking him questions I could not ask of a total stranger, etc. I might also see him differently now. But this change of aspect cannot be described in terms of an 'inner picture' (see Wittgenstein, 1963, p. 196).

A follower of Skinner, an American psychologist, Willard Day (1977), argues quite rightly that the knowledge or recognition evaded in self-deception has to be understood in terms of the person's *ability* to say and do certain things, and to respond in certain ways to particular situations. Knowledge is not a state of mind. Day is right in opposing the idea that a response must be mediated by an intervening state of recognition or understanding. However, he wrongly concludes that although it is commonly said that a person 'understands, or senses, or knows . . . in most cases this is likely to be mentalism'. This is a *non sequitur*. A state mediating between the environment and the response has to be rejected as a confused account of what it means to understand or to make sense. But to think that this is to reject the understanding itself, to claim that it plays no role in a person's response to his environment, is to identify the understanding with the state rejected and so to share the very misconception central to 'mentalism', 'introspectionism', 'Cartesianism', 'cognitivism', or whatever else one may choose to call it.

My point is this. To say, for instance, that when a person obeys a command there is no intervening mental process of understanding between the words he hears and what he does is one thing; to say that such a person acts without understanding is quite another. Skinner frequently slips from the former to the latter. The latter claim is objectionable in that it assimilates what happens when a person is given an order which he obeys to the pressing of a button which makes a bell ring. Skinner analyses the understanding of the language in which the order is given in terms of operant conditioning; and this will not do.

What Skinner says about the conception of mental states as 'mediators' or 'intervening variables' and his reasons for rejecting them are ambiguous and confused. He sometimes speaks of them as sheer epi-phenomena which can be ignored. At other times he speaks of them as a middle link in a causal chain where the first term is the stimulus and the last term is the response, claiming that it is enough to establish the inductive relation between the first and last terms. So we need not concern ourselves with the middle term; it is not a relevant factor in a functional analysis (see *SHB*, Ch. 3, section: ' A Functional Analysis'). He writes in this vein in the chapter on emotion:

> As long as we conceive of the problem of emotion as one of inner states, we are not likely to advance a practical technology. It does not help in the solution of a practical problem to be told that some feature of a man's behaviour is due to frustration or anxiety; we also need to be told how the frustration or anxiety has been induced and how it may be altered. In the end, we find ourselves dealing with two events — the emotional behaviour and the manipulable conditions of which that behaviour is a function — which comprise the proper subject matter of the study of emotion. (ibid., p. 167)

So sometimes Skinner speaks of these so-called 'mediating states' as real but of no value to a science of behaviour: 'These things are mental, but they offer no explanation and stand in the way of a more effective analysis' ('Behaviourism at Fifty', p. 80). At other times he speaks as if they are not even real: 'We do not feel the things which have been invented to explain behaviour' (*BFD*, p. 21).

3. Skinner's conception of a mental residue in a behaviouristic psychology and its privacy

This is extremely unsatisfactory and confused. Skinner talks here of 'the world within our skin'. His view is reminiscent of that of Hobbes and shares its ambiguities.

'The objection to inner states is not that they do not exist, but that they are not relevant in a functional analysis' *SHB*, p. 35). He means 'mental states', which he regards as 'intervening states'. He says:

> We do, indeed, feel things inside our skin, but we do not feel the things which have been invented to explain behaviour . . . We do feel certain states of our bodies associated with behaviour, . . . they are by-products and not to be mistaken for causes. (*BFD*, p. 21)

When Skinner speaks of 'the world within our skin' is this expression to be taken literally or metaphorically?

He says that the inner states which exist but are not relevant in a functional analysis are mental states. He also says that behaviourism does not reject 'private events'. (Thus Chapter 17 in *Science and Human Behaviour* is entitled 'Private Events in a Natural Science'.) If what he is referring to are 'physiological events', events that take place literally within our skin, would he have referred to them as 'private'? He might have in the sense that each person has a way of knowing, though not one that is foolproof, for instance, that he has a bad tooth, which others don't have. But though this could be described as a 'private' way of knowing the state of my own tooth, it is not one which it is inconceivable for another person to share, through something like an artificial nervous connection. So if this is what he meant, his use of the word 'private', though appropriate, would not be so attractive. Moreover, when Skinner writes that 'our joys, sorrows, loves and hates are peculiarly our own' (p. 257), he must know that our teeth and our internal organs are not in this sense peculiarly our own. After all, people wear dentures and, these days, they have other people's kidneys and hearts transplanted into them. So someone may say, 'I cannot have your pains, joys and sorrows in the sense that I can have your kidneys and heart.' But what does this mean? I do not think that Skinner is clear about this (see Dilman, 1975, Part II, Chs. 6 and 7).

These considerations pull one towards a metaphorical interpretation of Skinner's words, 'the world within our skin'. On the other hand there are other considerations that incline one to think that he meant them literally. In 'Behaviourism at Fifty' he says that 'what a man feels as anxiety may be autonomic reactions to threatening stimuli' (p. 95). Here it looks as if Skinner thinks of 'feel' as a perceptual verb, as in 'I felt the top of the table with my hand.' Thus he may be saying that, for example, when we say that we feel anxious what we feel are certain contractions in our stomach, and it is these that are 'private events', 'events within our skin'. But if by 'private' he means 'limited accessibility', as he says he does, then it is not true that what goes on within my stomach, or what happens to it, is private. It can be observed by X-ray or by means of a special instrument artificially inserted into my stomach. The passage I quoted earlier from *Beyond Freedom and Dignity* supports the literal interpretation: 'We do, indeed, feel things inside our own skin . . . We do feel certain states of our bodies associated with behaviour' (p. 21).

The same ambiguity runs through Chapter 17 in *Science and*

Human Behaviour. There he starts by talking of an inflamed tooth — a physical state of my body. He says that it is 'uniquely accessible' to the person whose tooth it is — like the events that take place within him during emotional excitement, for instance, accelerated heartbeat (p. 257). But as Professor Wisdom once remarked, 'The market-place would not be made private by my having a private way to it' (1952, p. 119). At the top of the next page Skinner talks of 'the stimulating *effect* of an inflamed tooth'. He says that it is not 'essentially different from that of, say, a hot stove' (p. 258). The stove, he says, is capable of affecting more than one person, the tooth is not. He then says that 'the stimulation from a tooth is an *inference* rather than a directly observable fact' (ibid.). But it is not clear how he uses the word 'stimulation'. That a person is 'stimulated' (to use the verb form) is just as publicly observable or unobservable in the case of the tooth as it is in the case of the stove, depending on what one means by 'stimulation'. If one means 'nervous processes', then there is no difference in this respect between the two cases. And if one means 'having sensations', then again there is no difference. When Skinner says that the stimulation of a tooth is an *inference* he is probably talking of the sensation. He is saying that we can observe that the stove is hot by touching it, by feeling it with our hand; but we cannot observe that someone's tooth hurts.

What a mess Skinner's thinking is in! Of course we can observe that someone's tooth hurts, that he is in pain. But notice that from one page to the next Skinner has slipped from talking of an inflamed tooth to the pain that a person feels in his tooth. If the pain can be said to be inside the skin in a literal sense, in this case inside the mouth, this is not to say that it is identical with the painful spot. So even if it is true that I may have pains in parts of my body that are inside my skin, in my inner organs, those pains are *not* inside my skin in the sense in which my internal organs are inside my skin.

Although evidently Skinner is confused on this point, he does not really identify the pain with the organ in question. If he did, he would not speak of it as known by *inference* by other people. He does so at the end of the chapter. He drops the ambiguous expressions 'stimulating effect of an inflamed tooth' and 'stimulation from a tooth', and he speaks openly of 'sensation'. The present analysis, he writes, in contrast with an 'operational definition of sensation',

continues to deal with the private event, even if only as an inference. It does not substitute the verbal report from which the inference is made for the event itself. The verbal report is a response to the private event and may be used as a source of information about it . . . We may avoid the dubious conclusion that . . . the verbal report . . . *is* the sensation. (p. 282)

Despite Skinner's claim to the contrary, this position is incompatible with any form of behaviourism. It is, in fact, the classical Cartesian position. Wittgenstein's account, which is not behaviouristic, though it is developed in criticism of the Cartesian position, would have been a much less damaging position for Skinner to adopt, and more in harmony with Skinner's thought.

Wittgenstein, in contrast with the classical behaviourist position, does not identify the words 'I am in pain' with the person's pain. Nor does he think of them as a 'report'. They are the verbal expression of pain. They are on a par with the primitive behavioural expression of pain, except for the difference that the latter is 'natural', 'instinctive' or 'animal', while the former is 'learned'. Wittgenstein speaks of this as learning to substitute one for the other. Ironically, Wittgenstein's account is more at home in Skinner's thought than Skinner's own account of the matter.

4. Skinner's view of emotions

If we take this dualistic interpretation of Skinner's view of the 'mental residue in a behaviouristic psychology', emotions become sensations or bodily feelings, stimulated by the bodily disturbances characteristic of the emotions. Thus when someone insults us and we strike him back in anger, the insult is the direct cause of our striking the other person. The anger we feel is nothing but the sensations caused by the physiological changes in our body: 'We do feel certain states of our bodies associated with behaviour . . . They are by-products and not to be mistaken for causes' (*BFD*, p. 21). Here what we feel are 'states of our bodies', the feelings are 'states of consciousness'. This view is similar to the James-Lange theory of emotions and may be represented as shown in the figure on the next page.

Notice that Skinner reduces (1) the insult to a physical stimulus and explains its power in terms of conditioning, (2) the behaviour to a reflex response, and (3) the emotion to a sensation. A state of

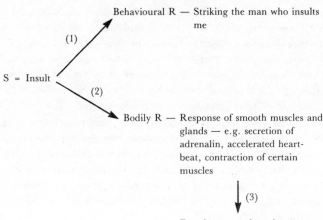

Behavioural R — Striking the man who insults me

(1)

S = Insult

(2)

Bodily R — Response of smooth muscles and glands — e.g. secretion of adrenalin, accelerated heart-beat, contraction of certain muscles

(3)

Emotion as a mirror-image or shadow cast in one's consciousness by the bodily disturbances — much in the way that a toothache is of the decayed state of one's tooth.

consciousness (which he says behaviourism does not ignore) is for Skinner nothing more than a sensation or bodily feeling. This directly contradicts his opposition to a cognitivist mythology of cognitive states. It is a grossly inadequate analysis of the angry man's state of consciousness. For if you ask such a person what he is conscious of in his anger, he will tell you that he is conscious of the insult under which he is smarting, of the withering look of the person who insulted him and of wanting to retaliate, to teach him a lesson.

The common-sense view of the matter is very different and is the one elaborated by Köhler. This is how I would represent the matter:

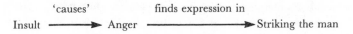

Insult —— 'causes' ——→ Anger —— finds expression in ——→ Striking the man

That is, our anger is a response to the insult which takes the form of wanting to retaliate in kind, and striking is the execution of it.

The insult, to begin with, is not a physical state of affairs. It cannot be reduced to a pattern of physical occurrences acting as stimuli. On this Gestalt psychologists are absolutely right. What the man tells you is an insult in particular circumstances, given the social milieu in which the interaction takes place. Its significance has a social origin; and what is said assumes that significance in particular circumstances. This is the first point.

Second, the connection between the insult and the emotional response may be characterised as 'causal'. But it is not like pulling the trigger of a gun and causing an explosion. The relation is an internal one. This is connected with the first point, namely that the insult is not a physical phenomenon, it cannot be reduced to a pattern of sounds which, through conditioning, have acquired the power of a stimulus. My anger in this case *is* or *involves* my grasp of the other man's words as an insult. That is, this grasp is *internal* to the anger I feel. My anger is a special mode of this grasp. The causation in question is not mechanical causation.

As Köhler (1929) puts it:

> When a sudden event is felt as producing fright in me, there arises a vehement impulse to move away from the locus of that event. This tendency is *experienced* as being the direct outcome of the startling occurrence, quite as much as the fright itself is *felt as* its direct result.

Köhler says that here the subject has *insight* into '*how* the tendency grows directly out of the nature of the situation' (p. 292). By 'the nature of the situation' Köhler means the situation as the subject sees it or thinks of it. The nature in question is what the subject makes of the situation. The tendency of the subject to move away from the situation in question is part of, internal to, or an expression of the fear he feels. This tendency has reference to the situation which is frightening him; that is, it cannot be described without reference to the situation as he sees it. In this sense, the tendency which he experiences contains, is internally directed or has 'intensional reference' to the situation which gives rise to it. It is in this sense that the causality (giving rise to) in question is an internal relation, and the subject grasps this relation non-inductively, that is without recourse to his experience of past instances when similar situations gave rise to similar tendencies in him. It is this non-inductive grasp which Köhler refers to as 'insight'.

What Köhler has to say about the relation between anger and its behavioural expressions and about how the emotion can be seen by others in these expressions is, I think, along the right lines.

The only other thing left to comment on in this connection are the *bodily disturbances* involved in emotions — pallor, shortness of breath, accelerated heartbeat, sweating, etc. Of course, these do not occur with every emotion one feels. But when they do occur they contribute to the characteristic flavour of the way the subject apprehends the object of his emotion (what he fears, what enrages him) and give urgency to the inclination at the heart of the emotion (to retaliate, to mourn, to commiserate, to make amends, to dance with joy, to run away). William James said that without the 'bodily states' the subject's perception of what is dangerous, joyful, sad, infuriating, attractive, repulsive, would remain purely cognitive, intellectual. We could say that when moved a person believes with more than his mind. He enters into the reality which the danger, the insult, the loss of a loved one, a misfortune, a triumph, a success has for him, with all his body. He not only enters into it, but affirms it.

5. The asymmetrical logic of the mind

What is in question here is a person's unique relation (1) to his own feelings and desires, which gives him a right to answer questions about what he feels and wishes and which no one can have without being him, and (2) to his own actions as a willing agent, so that he can say what he will do or intends to do without needing to have any evidence, like other people. In the first case, we speak of the feelings and desires as being his. Here we should note the difference between first-person verbal expressions and third-person statements or interpretations. In the second case, we speak of the agent's point of view as opposed to that of the observer.

Skinner shows no recognition of any of this. He speaks as if a person is an object of observation and manipulation to himself. In the following passage, for instance, he does not recognise that each person has a way of answering a question about his purpose or about what he proposes to do which no one else has, that his answer to such a question is not based on evidence and past experiences:

> Nor can our subject see his own purpose without reference to similar events . . . He may be in an advantageous position in describing these variables because he has had extended contact with his own behaviour for many years. But his statement

is not therefore in a different class from similar statements made by others who have observed his behaviour upon fewer occasions. (*SHB*, p. 88)

Let me quote Professor Malcolm's comment on this passage in 'Behaviourism as a Philosophy of Psychology':

The truth is that when a man tells you his purpose in doing something his statement is in a different class from a statement made by somebody else on the basis of observation of him. If you see someone rummaging about in the papers on his desk, and remember that when he had done this on previous occasions the rummaging had come to an end when he grabbed hold of his spectacles, you might reasonably conclude on these grounds that he is now looking for his spectacles.[1] But it would be weird if *he* were to reason as follows: 'Here I am rummaging about on my desk. When I have done this in the past my activity has terminated when I have caught hold of my spectacles. Therefore, I am probably looking for my spectacles'! If you heard a man make such a remark and believed that he was not joking, you would thereafter regard him with suspicion, because of the craziness of the remark. (1977 [1964], pp. 98–9)

As Malcolm puts it further on, first-person utterances like 'I am hungry', 'I am looking for my glasses', 'I intend to go home' (i) 'are not, for the most part, made on the basis of any observation'; (ii) 'in many cases they cannot be "tested" by checking them against physical events and circumstances other than the subject's own testimony'. A man's 'own testimony has a privileged status in respect of this sort of information about himself, and *not* "because he has had an extended contact with his own behaviour for many years" ' (p. 102). He says that behaviourism 'mistakenly assumes that when a man tells you what he wants, intends, or hopes, what he says is based on observation and, therefore, he is speaking about himself as if he were an *object of his own observation*' (pp. 102–3).

Skinner thinks that a man's relation to his own actions is not different from his relation to somebody else's actions. He had chastised Descartes and his followers for inventing an inner man and regarding him 'as driving the body very much as the man at the steering wheel drives the car' (*SHB*, p. 29). Ironically this is precisely how he, himself, regards a man's relation to his own actions, though he does not talk of an inner man. Thus in his chapter on self-control he writes:

> When a man controls himself, chooses a course of action, thinks out the solution to a problem, or strives towards an increase in self-knowledge, he is *behaving*. He controls himself precisely as he would control the behaviour of anyone else — through the manipulation of variables of which behaviour is a function. (p. 208)

All the examples that Skinner gives of self-control are of the same kind; they involve treating oneself as a third person, as a weak or naughty child — one hides a bottle or locks it and throws away the key in order to stop drinking; one draws the curtains in order to avoid distraction, one gets oneself into a good mood, perhaps even takes a pep-pill, before a trying appointment; one bites one's tongue to stop laughing; one hides the knives in the house to avoid committing suicide; and so on. These are not examples of self-control, of course, but of symptoms of its having broken down.

As for Skinner's analysis of decision and resolution, it is a caricature of what we mean. We make a prediction about our own behaviour and then arrange for that prediction to come true — arrange that we shall not want to depart from it, or even that we shall be ashamed to do so (see *SHB*, p. 237). I shall return to this.

My point is that in the two kinds of case Skinner represents people as treating themselves as *objects*, or as other people — which is not the same thing, except that in Skinner's psychology they come to the same thing, since other people are seen as objects to be controlled and manipulated. When I say that he represents people as treating themselves as objects, I mean objects of observation and manipulation.

6. Summary

So much for what Skinner rejects under the first heading — the mind and its states and the asymmetrical logic of the mind — his reduction of emotions to sensation, his quasi-Cartesian treatment of the inner dimension of the mind. I have commented on his treatment of first-person verbal expressions such as 'I am in pain',

'I am angry' as observational reports, contrasting Skinner's view with that of Wittgenstein. I have also pointed out a serious ambiguity in what he says about 'mental states'. On one hand he does something creditable, namely rejects a conceptual mythology which may be referred to as 'the intellectualist fallacy', while on the other he develops an epi-phenomenological account of the mind which reduces our joys, sorrows, loves and hates to mere sensations. Only he doesn't recognise the difference. The latter is part of his 'environmentalism', in which all mental explanations are rejected in favour of operant conditioning. As such, what is in question runs into our second heading of what Skinner rejects.

Notes

1. The example is Skinner's; see *SHB*, p. 90. Skinner's anlysis of 'I am looking for my glasses' is 'I have lost my glasses, I shall stop what I am doing when I find my glasses'.

4

Skinner's Reductive Analyses: Final Causes

1. Purpose and intention

Here, too, Skinner is very close to Hobbes, who claimed that 'all final causes are efficient causes', and that there is no place in a scientific psychology for any reference to purposes, goals and intentions. Skinner castigates 'almost everyone who is concerned with human affairs' for continuing to attribute intentions, purposes, aims and goals to human beings in explaining their behaviour. He writes: 'Statements which use such words as "incentive" or "purpose" are usually reducible to statements about operant conditioning' (*SHB*, p. 87). And: 'Purpose . . . is a way of referring to controlling variables' (ibid., p. 88). Again: 'One who readily engages in a given activity is not showing an interest, he is showing the effect of reinforcement' (ibid., p. 72).

For Skinner to say that a man is putting his shoes on with the *intention* of going for a walk means that he is doing what he has done in the past before going for a walk. This will not do at all. But the greatest difficulty it raises is for first-person declarations of intention. For here a person announces his intention without needing to have any grounds for what he says. Such declarations are not reports or predictions, they are not based on past experience. We have already seen that Skinner does not appreciate this. He does not see that there is any intrinsic difference between first- and third-person statements of intention:

The subject himself [he says] may be in an advantageous position in describing these variables [the variables to which, according to Skinner, we refer when we attribute a purpose or

intention to ourselves or to other people] [only] because he
has had an extended contract with his own behaviour for
many years. But his statement is not, therefore, in a different
class from similar statements made by others who have
observed his behaviour upon fewer occasions. (ibid., p. 88)

As he puts it in *Beyond Freedom and Dignity*: 'A person acts intentionally . . . not in the sense that he possesses an intention which
he then carries out, but in the sense that his behaviour has been
strengthened by consequences' (p. 108).

But a person who acts intentionally does have an intention
which he carries out. True, the Cartesian analysis of this as a
'psychic cause', that is a mental state which precedes the action
and causes it, will not do. For an intention need not be anything
separate from the action; it may be *in* the action. But even when it
is something that precedes the action, something that need not
issue in the action at all (since the person may change his mind and
give up his intention), it is still not something externally related to
the action. Furthermore, an intention is indeed a teleological
notion. Skinner rejects it partly on this score, his rejection of it
being programmatic — he rejects it because it does not fit his programme. When he writes 'a person who acts intentionally' he
means 'a person who we describe as acting intentionally' — the
first-person plural pronoun referring to the unenlightened.

In rejecting purpose and intention Skinner inevitably takes a
conception of human action and motivation which does violence to
our understanding of these things. His reason for treating that
understanding lightly and with contempt is nothing more than that
intention and purpose have no place in his scientific programme
for psychology. I should have thought that this is a reason for
viewing the scientific programme in question with suspicion, not
for taking our understanding of human behaviour lightly. The
success of such a programme in the field of physical phenomena is
not a sufficient reason for transferring it to the field of psychology.
The conceptual differences between the two fields constitute
weighty enough reasons for refraining from such an extension or
transfer.

Behind Skinner's theory of motivation as operant reinforcement
and aversion lies, thinly disguised, a Benthamite hedonism of the
crassest kind. In fact I would say that Skinner's theory of motivation is a form of psychological hedonism in modern dress. It recognises nothing other than the stick and the carrot as capable of

moving man. In his conception man is a creature who is not capable of responding to or being moved to action by anything else. All the rich variety of considerations that move men is represented by Skinner as forms of the carrot and the stick, positive and negative reinforcers. I shall say more about this later. My point now is that if, in the name of science, one wishes to reject teleology, then out goes with it our rich vocabulary for talking about human action and motivation. The consequence is that one can no longer bring into focus the reality which that vocabulary is used to talk about, namely human life as we know and live it.

Skinner, we have seen, wishes to combine an emphasis on the role of the *consequences* of behaviour in determining it with a *causal* account, one that avoids any mention of expectations on one hand and intentions on the other. He does this by talking of the causal relation between past consequences and the probability of a certain piece of behaviour measured in terms of its frequency over a period of time. In this way he can talk of consequences but avoid any reference to the future in explaining behaviour. So in the name of causality he denies that human conduct can be directed to the future: 'The fact that operant behaviour seems to be "directed toward the future" is misleading' (*SHB*, pp. 88–9). Later, writing about instances of people taking avoiding action, he says, 'That the behaviour of avoidance appears to be "directed" toward a future event may be explained as in operant behaviour in general: it is always past occurrences of conditioned negative reinforcers and past instances of their reduction which are responsible for the probability of the escape response' (p. 176).

Animals that have been fed regularly expect to be fed at a certain time of the day. I have no compunction about talking of an expectation here, and an expectation is necessarily directed to the future. Supposing that the animal in question is a dog, that he gets hungry at the time when he usually gets his food, and that he comes to the place where he is normally fed, looking for food. I would say that there is a minimal sense in which such behaviour is directed toward the future. As I said before, the expectation here is *in* the behaviour. The dog does not think to himself, 'This is where I get my food so I had better stand there, seeing that I am hungry.' Nor does he think, 'The food will be coming soon.' For the expectation to be thus detached from the behaviour, for it to motivate the behaviour through some sort of calculating or reasoning, it has to be formulated. This calls for language. So a creature who lacks the capacity for language cannot be thus motivated by a thought about the future. In this sense, the dog's behaviour is directed toward the future only in a minimal sense. What this comes to is this: The dog expects to be fed all right, but not because he reasons that this is the right time and the right place. His expectation is not mediated by reasoning; it is habitual. The answer to 'Why does he expect food?' is 'Because this is the time when and the place where he has been fed before — regularly.' The expectation is an instance of the operation of habit.

Skinner, for no good reason, does not want to speak of 'expectation' and he describes the expectant behaviour as 'operant behaviour'. What he means is what I have described in plain language. But Skinner has too big a philosophical chip on his shoulder to go along with it. All the same, there is not too much substantive difference between our respective ways of understanding the dog's behaviour in the example I considered.

Examples of the ape's behaviour in Köhler's experiments are transitional cases which do not concern us now. But to say that the behaviour of human beings, who possess the ability to speak, and whose whole life has been transformed by this ability, is never directed towards the future is ludicrous. It is to suggest that human behaviour, which includes planning, making provisions for the future, carrying out various strategies and fully intentional actions, is not different from the dog's behaviour in our example.

Wittgenstein wrote, 'We say a dog is afraid his master will beat him; but not, he is afraid his master will beat him tomorrow. Why not?' (*Inv.*, Sec. 650). And again: 'A dog believes his master is at the door. But can he also believe his master will come the day after tomorrow? And *what* can he not do here? How do I do it?' (p. 174). Skinner has not really thought about these questions. Smug in his belief that outside science everything is prejudice, animism, and superstition, he has rushed in where angels fear to tread. But, of course, the belief that outside science everything is prejudice and superstition is not itself a scientific idea, and it cannot be justified by any of the methods of science.

2. Intentionality and the future

Skinner, as we have seen, eschews all reference to *expectation*, but he does not deny all expectant behaviour. What he does is to assimilate it to the kind of example we have considered in connection with the dog.

An expectation is necessarily directed to the future; and this applies to all expectant behaviour. This *directedness* has come to be called 'intentionality' and has certainly been recognised in psychology by Brentano, by the Gestalt psychologist Köhler, and by philosophers — the names of Husserl, Sartre, and Wittgenstein come particularly to mind. I shall confine my remarks to Köhler.

For Köhler 'the visible behaviour of other human beings is closely connected with their mental states and offers an immediate basis for comprehension'. Indeed, a person's expectations can be wholly contained in his expectant behaviour and can be seen there by others. Similarly, Köhler holds that there is a comprehensible or intelligible relation between a so-called 'mental state', such as expectation, or the behaviour in which it is contained and where it can be seen by others, and what is expected, namely a future event. This relation is not an associative, experiential relation, as Skinner makes it out to be. It does not arise through the repeated binding together of material not previously bound together (Katz, 1979, Ch. 17).

For Skinner, in contrast, a man knows what he is expecting, or what he is about (e.g. that he is looking for his glasses, or that he is going to post a letter) on the basis of past experience. We cannot see that someone walking down the street intends to post a letter before seeing that he posts the letter, unless we have observed similar behaviour and similar consequences before. Nor can our subject see this in his own case without reference to similar events (*SHB*, p. 83).

For Skinner, then, the connection between a person's walking down the street at a certain time and his posting the letter he is carrying at a later time, a time in the future, is purely contingent. The two are connected only in the sense that on repeated occasions in the past one was followed by the other. In other words, there cannot be an 'intrinsic connection' between the two; what the man is doing now cannot be directed towards the future.

For Köhler it is otherwise, and surely he is right. I could be walking down the road with the intention of posting the letter I hold in my hand. The intention is not something additional to my walking, except in the sense that I could say beforehand that I am going to post a letter. Nor is what I say a prediction. I may change my mind and give up the intention, or I may be prevented from carrying it out, but what I say I intend to do is *internally related* to the intention I declare. That is why I can say what I am going to do without research or reflection. It is certainly not based on past experience as Skinner claims.

This question is discussed by Köhler in Chapter 10, 'Insight', of his book *Gestalt Psychology*. What he means by 'insight' is to be contrasted with 'inductive knowledge'. Inductive knowledge is based on experience, whereas what Köhler calls 'insight' is one's recognition of intrinsic, intelligible connections. He does not actually give the example of an intention. The examples he gives are admiration, enjoyment, fright, and effort.

Admiration is not something going on within me, he says, though not quite in these words. It is a 'directed' attitude — directed toward something or someone. So I cannot doubt whom it is I admire; nor is this something that I have to find out. When I enjoy a long, cool drink on a hot summer day, I do not have to learn what my pleasure refers to, what it is I am enjoying. As Köhler puts it, between the attitude (the enjoyment) and the cool drink 'we experience an "intrinsic" connection'.

In *The Analysis of Mind* (1949) Russell had said, 'The thing which will bring a restless condition to an end is said to be what is desired. But only experience can show what will have this sedative effect, and it is easy to make mistakes' (p. 23). This is the kind of view which Köhler is combating. Wittgenstein makes fun of it in his *Philosophical Remarks*: 'I believe Russell's theory comes to the following: . . . If I should like to eat an apple and someone gives me a punch in the stomach, so that the desire to eat goes away, then it was this punch that I wanted originally' (p. 64). Wittgenstein, like Köhler, argues that the relation between a desire and what is desired, an expectation and what is expected, an intention and what is intended is an *internal* relation. That is why, as Malcolm puts it in his review of *Philosophical Remarks*, 'I do not and cannot learn from experience what I expect.' Nor, normally, do I have to learn what it is that frightens me. I do not have to be frightened by something many times before I can say that *this* is what frightens me. As Köhler puts it, in metaphorical language, 'Fright is *experienced* as jumping at us right out of the very nature of certain definite events.'

He then gives the example where I have my arm stretched out horizontally, become tired after a while, and have to exert myself, to make an effort, to keep my arm in that position. The effort (he argues) is not sensations or feelings I receive from my muscles, ephi-phenomena, events under my skin (as Skinner would describe them). It is something I do and it has a 'direction' — it has as its object keeping my arm upraised. He refers to David Hume and the way he conceives of the will as an internal phenomenon externally, causally connected with an external movement. 'What a strange argument!' he says.

When I keep my arm up in this way, despite the tiredness I feel, when I run away from something I am afraid of, when I turn away from from something that disgusts me, when I get up from my place with the intention of saying good-bye and going home, what I do has a *direction*. As Köhler puts it, I do not only experience the result, but also the 'why' and the 'how' in the particular context. It is this which he calls 'insight'.

Skinner had said that the man who is on his way to post a letter 'has had an extended contact with his own behaviour for many years' and that it is this that enables him to say that he is going to post a letter. Köhler, in contrast, argues that what this man says when he says what he intends to do is not based on anything. It certainly does not come from any extended contact the man has had with his own behaviour in the past.

3. Summary

Let me repeat two points I have made in this discussion.

1. A person's relation to his own actions, present and future, is radically different from that of other people. What he says about them is in a different class, has a different status, from what other people say about his actions. This is what I referred to as the 'asymmetrical logic of the mind' (after Wisdom, 1952). It is connected with the 'internal relation' there is between an intention and the action intended, between what I am doing with a certain intention now and the way I follow it up. That internal relation is an instance of Köhler's 'intentional relation' between what he calls 'mental attitudes' and their objects. In the case of intentions and the actions which embody them we can speak of this relation as their 'directedness toward the future'.

2. Skinner denies this by representing all human motivation as species of 'operant conditioning'. Thus he assimilates the example of a man looking for his glasses in the drawer to the case of a pigeon who has been conditioned, by being given food, to peck a spot on the wall of a box after the spot has been removed. 'Must we say [he asks] that the pigeon is "looking for the spot"?' (*SBH*, p. 89). The innuendo is: The man is no more looking for his glasses than the pigeon is doing so. His behaviour is not

directed toward the future; it is the result of past environmental contingencies.

5

Skinner's Reductive Analyses: the Self, Self-control, the Will, Decision and Action

Skinner speaks of the self as a fiction. The concept of self, he says, is not essential in an analysis of behaviour. It is simply a device for representing a functionally unified system of responses.

Here, too, he runs together the terms in which we think about ourselves and our behaviour and a certain philosophical account which he confuses with animism: 'The self is most commonly used as a hypothetical cause of action' (*SHB*, p. 283). We have seen the sense in which Descartes held such a view and what it amounts to. It is not the same thing as thinking of the wind as being blown by Aeolus, or of the rain as being cast down by Jupiter Pluvius. In any case, can one trust Skinner's understanding of what Greek deities meant to the early Greeks when his understanding of what Christian beliefs mean to Christians is so crude? Nor is rejecting the Cartesian philosophical model for the self the same thing as shifting our attention from a fictitious 'originating agent within the organism' to 'external variables' which control human behaviour.

It is the latter that represents the focus of Skinner's interest. For what he is concerned with is replacing the kind of agency exemplified in human actions, and the possibility of autonomy, with a thoroughgoing 'environmentalism'. His view is that a man is always and ultimately acted on. He reacts, but he never acts — not on his own behalf:

As more and more of the behaviour of the organism has come to be explained in terms of stimuli, the territory held by inner explanations has been reduced. The 'will' has retreated up the spinal cord, through the lower and then the higher part of the brain, and finally, with the conditioned reflex, has escaped through the front of the head. At each stage, some part of the control of the organism has passed from a hypothetical inner entity to the external environment. (*SHB*, pp. 48–9)

There is, of course, a distinction between doing something and making or forcing oneself to do it, and between not doing something and refraining from doing it, as when one resists a temptation — in short between acting in the ordinary sense of 'intentional action' and exercising self-control. Skinner's account of both is deeply defective.

We begin with self-control. For Skinner what is involved here is the use of various techniques by a person, for example, to resist a temptation. He thinks of it as a form of self-manipulation. To quote some of his examples: A person leaves most of his pocket money at home to avoid spending it. Another puts a box of chocolates out of sight to avoid overeating. A mother seals her own lips with adhesive tape to keep herself from nagging her child. To control his anger a man simply walks away. I am inclined to say that these are not really instances of self-control. For instance, the angry man walks away because he is unable to control his anger, the mother seals her lips with adhesive tape because she cannot check herself from nagging her child.

Skinner refers to the behaviour which constitutes the application of such techniques as the 'controlling response', and he says that it consists of the manipulation of variables in which the controlled response is a function. The picture is that of a musical instrument manipulating its own stops. This, obviously, raises the question of what manipulates the manipulation — who controls the controlling response? Skinner's answer is that ultimately society is responsible for the larger part of the behaviour of self-control. He has in mind education, what he calls 'ethical training', which he analyses in terms of operant conditioning. So, he says, 'little ultimate control remains with the individual'. He goes on:

A man may spend a great deal of time designing his own life . . . Such activity appears to exemplify a high order of self-determination. But it is also behaviour and we account for it in terms of other variables in the environment and history of the individual. It is these variables which provide the ultimate control. (*SHB*, p. 240)

So self-control is accountable in the end in terms of variables

38

outside the individual himself, which means that what we call 'self-control' is not really self-control — just as the man who describes himself as looking for his glasses is no more looking for his glasses than Skinner's pigeon is looking for the spot which has been removed from the place it is pecking. Skinner adds, 'An analysis which appeals to external variables makes the assumption of an inner originating and determining agent unnecessary' (ibid., p. 241).

Skinner's account of intentional action and decision is similar to his account of self-control. In fact, he cannot distinguish between doing something and making oneself do it. Decision for him is the manipulation of variables: 'The individual sometimes does this [i.e. makes a decision] by manipulating some of the variables of which his behaviour is a function' (p. 242). For instance, 'we may decide about the vacation *by* making a down-payment to hold a reservation' (p. 243). This is not a slip. Skinner thinks of making the down-payment as a *means* of making a decision. In his view we bring off the decision by making the down-payment.

But this is absurd. Deciding to do something, intending to do something for the future, is not making ourselves do it, binding ourselves to do it, tying ourselves down or putting ourselves, as it were, on a railroad track. We do sometimes do this. Afraid that we shall not go on the holiday which will please the children, because we are attracted by an alternative arrangement, we make the down-payment well ahead of the time when it is due. It is because we do not trust ourselves to make the right decision or to keep to it that we thus bind ourselves. But this is the exception and not the rule. Besides it is an instance of forcing oneself to do something, not of taking a decision.

According to Skinner, making the down-payment is introducing a new variable which controls the behaviour. But in that case I would be going on the holiday, partly at least, because I wouldn't want to lose the down-payment I had made. I would be going to avoid the consequences that would ensue if I did not go. As Skinner puts it, 'We prepare aversive stimuli which will control our own future behaviour when we make a resolution' (*SHB*, p. 237). This is so, according to Skinner, not only in the case of making the down-payment, but also when I say, 'I will do such-and-such':

This is essentially a prediction concerning our own behaviour. By making it in the presence of people who supply aversive stimuli when a prediction is not fulfilled, we arrange consequences which are likely to strengthen the behaviour resolved upon. Only by behaving as predicted can we escape the aversive consequences of breaking our resolution. (ibid.)

What a travesty!

As with Skinner's account of self-control, however, the problem reappears with regard to our introducing the variable: You decide about the vacation *by* making a down-payment, decide on making the down-payment by filling in and signing a notice of withdrawal from your interest account, and so on. Skinner brings this series to a close by denying our ultimate responsibility for what we do. So ultimately our descisions are made for us; we do not really decide. Skinner's account of decision is, therefore, paradoxical. If taking a decision were a matter of manipulating variables which control our behaviour, this would presuppose that the choice was already made. Our manipulation of this or that variable would not be the making of the decision, but putting it into effect, executing it.

I would say that 'making a down-payment to hold a reservation' is, given particular circumstances, an *expression* of my decision to go on a holiday. Indeed, it is true that when I take a decision, when I say, 'We shall go on that holiday,' or when I make a down payment, I *commit myself for the future*. This is at the centre of our notion of an intention, a resolution, a decision. Skinner might say, 'I commit myself by making the down-payment.' This is true, provided we understand the notion of commitment correctly, as Skinner does not. I would rather say, 'commit myself *in* making the down-payment'. I equally commit myself when I say, 'We shall go on that holiday.' These are all expressions of the decision. Deciding *is* committing myself for the future in a certain way; so is making the down-payment. Hence making the down-payment *is* the decision, or an *expression* of the decision.

Skinner, on the other hand, thinks of it as the manipulation of variables that control my behaviour in a way that will ensure that I go on the holiday. He thinks of this as a kind of influence I exert on my own future behaviour. This view about what it means to make a decision and Skinner's view of my declaration of an intention as a prediction based on past experience of my own behaviour are two sides of the same coin.

I can commit myself for the future in many ways: in making the down-payment, in saying that I will go, in promising my wife. Such commitment is not a *means* of carrying out an intention, a way of ensuring that I will do something. It is not a form of manipulation. But this misunderstanding seems to be widespread in psychology. Nor is it confined to behaviourism (see, for instance, Mischel and Mischel, 1977; Secord, 1977).

It is interesting that Secord's account of commitment is riddled with the same misunderstandings that we find in Skinner's account of decision. All the examples he gives parallel those of Skinner. For, like Skinner, he runs together 'commitment' and what he calls 'constraining conditions':

> A constraining condition may be a form of giving up options to behave in certain ways . . . Consider the murderer who begs to be put in prison so that he won't commit any more murders; or . . . the individual who leaves home without cigarettes or money in his pocket so that he won't smoke. (p. 267)

Or take the man I mentioned before who hides all sharp instruments in the kitchen because he is subject to suicidal impulses. This is not *undertaking* not to kill himself in the sense of 'undertaking' or 'commitment' involved in a decision. It is simply making it difficult to do something which he is clearly against doing at the time, lest at a later time he is subject to an impulse that clouds his vision so that he is unable to summon considerations that do normally weigh with him. Such a man is not deciding not to kill himself when he is subject to a suicidal impulse; he is not committing himself for the future. He is taking steps that will ensure that he is unable to go along when he is subject to the impulse and finds it overwhelming.

Secord asks why promises are kept and he answers: because once they are made they are costly to break. So he speaks of commitment (which he identifies with 'constraining conditions') as a *means* of carrying out an intention: 'Commitment helps people to carry out their intentions' (p. 269). This is similar to the way Skinner sees making the down-payment. Secord does not see the difference between a man who keeps his word because he has given it, and for no other reason, and one who keeps it to avoid embarrassment or feeling bad. And neither does Skinner. He cannot understand how a man's word can be his bond, without reference to independent variables that control his behaviour.

Thus doing something for its own sake is still explained in terms of consequences that have to be reinforced. Skinner discusses this in a section entitled 'Generalised Reinforcers' (*SHB*, Ch. 5). In plain language, when one is said to do something for its own sake, in Skinner's book, one is not doing whatever is in question (e.g. playing a game of tennis, listening to music) because of what one finds in it, but because of what one gets out of it: 'We are automatically reinforced when we successfully control the physical world. This may explain our tendency to engage in skilled crafts, in artistic creation, and in such sports as bowling, billiards, and tennis' (ibid., p. 77). He always locates the reward for which we engage in an activity in its *consequences*, never in the activity itself. He does not see that the activity can be its own reward. This is not surprising when the word 'interest' has no place in Skinner's vocabulary: 'One who readily engages in a given activity [he writes in an earlier section] is not showing an interest, he is showing the effect of reinforcement' (p. 72).

Yet the difference between finding something in what one is doing and getting something out of it is crucial for understanding what it means to do something for its own sake. When one speaks of finding something in what one is doing, say reading poetry, one is referring to what one is doing — to what one is reading, namely the poetry. When, in contrast, one speaks of getting something out of it, one is referring to its effect on the subject — e.g. the satisfaction, the thrill. Thus when one finds an activity rewarding, it is what one finds in the activity that is at the centre of one's attention. This cannot be accounted for in terms of operant conditioning. Whereas when one finds its consequences rewarding it is the self that is at the centre of one's concern. One is moved, not by one's love of the activity, but by what it pays in terms of, for example, titillation, prestige, a sense of well-being, approval, a sense of control. These are all what Skinner calls 'generalised reinforcers'.

Skinner cannot understand how anyone could be moved to an action when there is not the prospect, the promise, the expectation of some sort of payment; or, if these words do not exist in his vocabulary, when he has not been reinforced by payments he has received in the past in the case of similar actions: 'To teach a child to read or sing we must work out a programme of educational reinforcement in which appropriate responses "pay off" frequently' (ibid., p. 74). 'We evaluate the strength of reinforcing events when we attempt to discover what someone is "geting out of life"' (ibid.). For Skinner what sustains a friendship can be no other than what a person gets out of his friend:

The behaviour of associating with a particular friend varies as the friend varies in supplying reinforcement. If we observe this covariation, we may then be fairly sure of 'what this friendship means' or 'what our subject sees in his friend'. (p. 74)

Obviously what he sees in his friend, according to Skinner, is what he can get out of him.

What this amounts to is that in Skinner's book people do not and cannot do things 'for their own sake' — study because of their interest in a subject, make genuine friendships, feel affection for others unless they get some return. Equally, he says, 'a person does not act for the good of others because of a feeling of belongingness'. He means, because the other man is his neighbour, or a human being. 'His behaviour depends upon the control exerted by the social environment.' Skinner means, because he is made to do so, because he has been conditioned by his 'moral training' to do so (*BFD*, p. 110). For Skinner, as for Polus in Plato's *Gorgias*, 'good' simply means 'rewarding', 'advantageous', or in Skinner's language, 'reinforcing': 'good things are positive reinforcers' (ibid., p. 103). For him 'the whole point of ethical training' is to reinforce certain forms of behaviour (*SHB*, p. 240). (See his analysis of value judgments, *SHB*, Ch. 28, §1, pp. 428–30; and *BFD*., Ch. 6, entitled 'Values'.)

I mentioned Skinner's rejection of the self as an 'inner core' (see Taylor, 1977, p. 57) from which men's overt actions flow, and of consciousness in the sense of intentionality (see Hampshire, 1959, pp. 94, 119), in favour of 'environmental variables which control human behaviour'. I mentioned his rejection of the notions of self-control and decision, and his misunderstanding of what it means to commit oneself for the future — a notion central to our concepts of intention, decision, promising and intentional action. I have also mentioned his inability to understand and accommodate instances where people are described as doing something for its own sake and of valuing something for itself. Not surprisingly, Skinner's account of what is voluntary in human behaviour is equally unsatisfactory.

Like Hobbes, Skinner claims that the distinction between what is voluntary and what is involuntary concerns only surface differences. What is in question here is not *who* is in control (he says), but what *kind* of control the behaviour is subject to. Voluntary behaviour is subject to operant conditioning, and involuntary behaviour is reflex behaviour — unconditioned as well as conditioned, in the Pavlovian sense. But voluntary behaviour is ultimately just as much subject to the environment as involuntary behaviour, only in a more subtle and indirect way (*SHB*, p. 112).

The distinction between voluntary and involuntary behaviour bears upon our changing concept of personal responsibility. We do not hold people responsible for their reflexes — e.g. for coughing in church. We hold them responsible for their operant behaviour — e.g. for whispering in church. But there are variables which are responsible for the whispering as well as for the coughing, and these may be just as inexorable. When we recognise this, we are likely to drop the notion of responsibility altogether and with it the doctrine of free will as an inner causal agent. (*SHB*, pp. 115–16)

6

Freedom of the Will

Given Skinner's reductive analyses and all that he throws away, his rejection of free will is not an additional feature in his account of behaviour. There is no place in his conceptual scheme for the notions of intentional action, decision, and self-control. Nor is there a place in it for the possibility of a person being guided by considerations of reason in his actions, or for a distinction between acting and thinking on one's own behalf and mere conformity. So the dice have already been loaded in favour of 'determinism'.

Once Skinner has settled this question, his arguments against free will are abstract and crude. I shall do little more than note them; they speak for themselves. As with most things Skinner rejects, his rejection of free will has a double aspect: On one hand he rejects a defective account of it, and on the other he rejects the thing itself — free will, the self, self-control, purpose, intention, or decision, as we normally understand these things. Since he cannot himself see any alternative to the account in question, he cannot reject it without rejecting that of which it is an account. He rejects it partly for this reason, and partly in the name of a scientific programme for psychology in which he sees no place for free will.

Skinner clearly thinks of free will as the power of an internal agency to interfere with causal relationships (*SHB*, p. 7). This internal agency, he says, is thought of as itself not subject to causality. Its actions are spontaneous and, therefore, random. This, he claims, is the traditional view, and it seems clear to him that it is at loggerheads with the scientific view. There is no doubt in his mind that the scientific view is correct and that the traditional view has to be abandoned. He points out that it is already being abandoned in connection with certain forms of human behaviour:

We sometimes exonerate a man by pointing to 'extenuating circumstances'. We no longer blame the uneducated for their ignorance or call the unemployed lazy. We no longer hold children wholly accountable for their delinquencies. The insane have long since been cleared of responsibility for their condition, and the kinds of neurotic or psychotic behaviour to which we now apply this extenuation are multiplying. (ibid., p. 8)

Thus, Skinner argues, we are in a state of transition from a traditional philosophy of human nature to a scientific point of view; we have accepted the assumption of determinism in part. The traditional and the scientific points of view dictate different and, indeed, opposite practices relating to the study of man and to our attitudes toward practical and moral problems, such as in the case of the treatment of offenders. Skinner himself clearly sees advantages in adopting a position which would favour one set of practices at both the theoretical and the practical levels.

Skinner's belief that all human behaviour is determined by operant conditioning is a form of determinism and excludes free will. He makes a dichotomy between the claim that all human behaviour is causally determined and the view that much of it is spontaneous (ibid., p. 24). Those who take the latter view are the astrologers and the alchemists of psychology. The scientific psychologist rejects the spontaneity of human behaviour and is concerned with investigating its causes. He wants to know why people behave as they do. By discovering and analysing these causes he can predict behaviour and control and manipulate it. The analysis belongs to scientific investigation and the control of what Skinner calls 'behavioural technology'. This technology is based on the science of behaviour, with operant conditioning as its cornerstone. It is the (largely social) environment which controls behaviour; not the person whose behaviour is in question. So men are not free.

This is how Skinner puts it in *Beyond Freedom and Dignity*:

Behaviour which operates upon the environment to produce consequences ('operant' behaviour) can be studied by arranging environments in which specific consequences are contingent upon it. The contingencies under investigation have become steadily more complex, and one by one they are taking over the explanatory functions previously assigned to personalities, states of mind, feelings, traits of character, purposes, and intentions. [This has practical results.] The environment can be manipulated. It is true that man's genetic endowment can be changed only very slowly, but changes in the environment of the individual have quick and dramatic effects. A technology of operant behaviour is . . . already well advanced and it may prove to be commensurable with our problems. (p. 24)

In his utopian novel, *Walden Two*, Skinner depicts the application of this technology in a small imaginary community in America for what he regards to be the good of the people and, ultimately, of all humanity.

Let me give a brief summary of what the chief character of the novel, the psychologist Frazier, Skinner's spokesman, has to say about freedom. He begins by denying the existence of freedom: 'I deny that freedom exists at all. You can't have a science about a subject matter which hops capriciously about.' One answer is that freedom is not the same thing as caprice. Another answer is that if freedom excludes the scientific study of human behaviour, then so much for such a study. But Castle, the philosopher, does not take either tack. He advances a counter-example. I am free, he says, to hold or drop these matches. Frazier's comment is that whichever Castle does, 'it was all lawful and you had no choice'. He adds: 'I didn't say that behaviour is always predictable.' But he does not say what law it might be obeying, nor does he give any reason for thinking that it does, or must, accord with some law. His claim comes to this: 'It accords with some law or other, even though I cannot tell you what that law is, nor can anyone else.' As such the claim is empty; an idle wheel which turns no mechanism.

Frazier goes on to say that when he says that men never act freely he does not mean that they never do what they want. He distinguishes between cases where men do what they want to do and cases where they do what they are forced to do. In the former there is no restraint, no revolt, and men *feel* 'free'. Yet Frazier's view is that here too men are *not* free. For they want what they have been *made* to want.

Men, he says, raise the question of freedom when there is restraint. But restraint is only *one* sort of control, and the absence of restraint is not freedom. When men *feel* free it is not control that is lacking, but the objectionable control of force. When men strike for freedom, they strike against oppression, that is the objectionable kind of control, the one that involves force. They never strike against the forces which made them want to act the way they do.

He adds that Walden Two is the freest place on earth. It is free precisely because we made no use of force or the threat of it. By skilful planning, by a wiser choice of techniques, we increase the *feeling* of freedom. It is not planning which infringes upon freedom, but planning which uses force. In the book Frazier is often made to face the charge of totalitarianism because everything in the community of Walden Two is controlled down to the smallest detail. Frazier, like Skinner, is obsessed by control, and so he has to make a case that to abdicate control is not to make men freer. It is to leave them at the mercy of chance forces. In that case they are just as controlled.

The paradox which Frazier does not face is that the controller is only a vehicle of control, as much subject to control as those he controls. So how can he distinguish between what he calls 'rational control', which he boasts Walden Two illustrates, and arbitrary control? How can there be 'rational control' or planning where purpose does not exist, where intention is a will-o'-the-wisp? Skinner does not face up to these questions.

What we preserve (Frazier says) is a personal *sense* of freedom; our members are practically always doing what they want, what they 'choose' to do. He puts 'choose' in inverted commas. But *we* see to it that they will want to do precisely the things that are *best* for themselves and their community. This is, of course, arrogance verging on megalomania. He concludes that their behaviour is determined, yet they are free.

He should have said: Yet they *feel* free. For Frazier, 'yet they are free' is a slip. For he is not a 'compatibilist'. If he were Hume he could have said what he says without contradiction. For Hume argues that there is no incompatibility between freedom and determinism. Determinism is the reign of causality and causality is not a form of compulsion. Freedom, on the other hand, is opposed to compulsion, not to causality.

All the same, Frazier's view has *some* affinity to Hume's. But Skinner's view does not, for he comes quite near to seeing human beings as puppets.

7

Skinner's Picture of Human Life and Human Nature

The conceptual surgery which Skinner performs in the name of a scientific psychology commits him to a view of human beings as near-puppets. But behind this conceptual framework there lurks that shallow picture which commercial advertisers generally paint of people as incapable of any deep feeling or conviction; caring for nothing except what glitters; as malleable as putty; responding only to what promises pleasure, comfort or some advantage, or to what threatens unpleasant consequences — reward and punishment, positive and negative reinforcement. Thus, for instance, his conception of what it is to like or enjoy music: 'It has been shown experimentally that people can "like" modern music if they listen to it while eating.' He adds: 'As advertisers well know, the responses and attitudes evoked by pretty girls, babies, and pleasant scenes may be transferred to trade names, products, pictures of products and so on' (*SHB*, p. 57).

In Skinner's view what moves people is either some form of payment or the fear of punishment. The role of interests, convictions, love, concern, and ideals in human life is either analysed away or grotesquely distorted. It is true that in *Walden Two* Frazier says, 'We don't attach an economic or honorific value to education. It has *its own value* or none at all.' And again: 'Geography, literature, etc. — our children learn them for *themselves*.' He contrasts education as it is practised in *Walden Two* with traditional conceptions of education: 'We don't need to create motives. We avoid the spurious academic needs. We appeal to the curiosity which is characteristic of the unrestrained child.' But there is no place for these ideas in Skinner's scheme, and Frazier's appeal to them is deceptive. We have already considered Skinner's analysis

49

of valuing something for itself and of doing something for its own sake, according to which what we value is a 'generalised reinforcer'. It is 'effective even though the primary reinforcers upon which it is based no longer accompany it' (*SHB*, p. 81). Thus in the case of the miser (one of Skinner's examples), money, which was originally valued as a means, that is, for what it can buy, comes to be valued as an end, or for itself.

This is a bad example. For it is not an example of something valued for itself. Yet by being made a model of valuing something for itself it serves to run together two very different kinds of case: for example, somebody interested in a particular academic subject because he has developed an interest in it and so sees in it what to an outsider may mean little, and somebody who has grown dependent on it, like an alcoholic on drinks, although he is indifferent to all the ulterior ends — prestige, power, advancement — for which someone else may pursue it. If these two academics are classified together and then contrasted with a third one who is interested, say, only in promotion, what is distinctive about the first academic will come to be obscured. For the differences that separate the first two are greater than those that separate the last two. In fact, the differences that separate the academic who is only at home in the world of his studies from the one who is only concerned with promotion are, from one point of view, more apparent than real. For he too is not really disinterested in the pursuit of his studies; it is what they do for him that attaches him to them. They feed his ego, or at least they afford it protection.

This has to be contrasted with the first case, where the studies nourish his soul. 'Feed the ego', 'nourish the soul' — I don't suppose that Skinner would see the difference — that is, even if he did not reject the terms out of hand as pure mythology. Thus, in another field, that concerning religious and spiritual matters, he classifies the hermit with the hippie and the hobo, describing them as 'drop-outs' — they drop out of a culture (*BFD*, p. 33). In *Science and Human Behaviour* he says, 'The hermit escapes from the control of the ethical group . . . as the boy runs away from home' (p. 359). Skinner cannot see anything in the hermit's quest for solitude except escapism, just as he cannot see anything in the disinterested pursuit of academic studies, except the reinforcement of an ivory tower.

In fact Skinner's analysis of valuing something for itself, modelled on the case of the miser described as valuing money or gold for itself, is simply John Stuart Mill in modern dress.

This is what Mill says:

> Virtue, according to the utilitarian doctrine, is not naturally
> and originally part of the end, but it is capable of becoming
> so, and in those who love it disinterestedly it has become so,
> and is desired and cherished, not as a means to happiness, but
> as part of their happiness. (1948, Ch. 4)

This is very similar to Skinner's doctrine of 'generalised
reinforcers'. Indeed Mill then goes on to illustrate what he means
with the example that Skinner gives, names the miser's love of
money. He concludes that 'from being a means to happiness, it
[the money] has come to be itself a principal ingredient of the
individual's conception of happiness'. Of course, what both Mill
and Skinner ignore is the difference between the miser's love of
money or gold and the way in which a truly virtuous and upright
person cares for justice and honesty.

Skinner's whole analysis of moral values, value judgements and
language (the way it is acquired and what it signifies) is grotesque.
For him 'That's right' means no more than 'Good boy!', as you
may say this to a dog who responds to your command 'Sit' (*SHB*,
p. 78). This belongs with his whole analysis of language and
understanding language:

> The verbal stimulus 'Come to dinner' is an occasion upon
> which going to a table and sitting down is usually reinforced
> with food. The stimulus comes to be effective in increasing
> the probability of that behaviour and is produced by the
> speaker because it does so. (ibid., p. 109)

That is, the response to the words is learned through reinforcement with food, and the speaker learns to utter the words through
reinforcement by his guest's response. That response is induced by
operant conditioning, as the secretion of saliva and gastric juices
on hearing the words 'Won't you come to dinner' is induced by
Pavlovian, respondent conditioning (ibid., p. 113). As Skinner
puts it, 'The whole field of verbal behaviour exemplifies the use of
stimuli in *personal control*' (ibid., p. 317).

Skinner's whole treatment of language and reasoning has close
affinities to the views expressed by the Greek sophist Gorgias,
criticised by Socrates in Plato's dialogue by that name. For
Gorgias, too, language is an instrument of manipulation, and

effectiveness in manipulation is all there is to understanding, whether of people or language. Sophists, Gorgias insists, teach you the skill of 'persuasion', of playing on the right stops. This is an inductive, experimental knack, and you don't have to learn anything about the subjects on which you are speaking in order to be able to use language effectively. For Skinner too, speaking is a *skill* (ibid., p. 408), and the effects of exercising it well are produced by operant conditioning. Learning to speak, like learning anything else, is a matter of being reinforced in certain responses — those favoured by the community. He is totally unaware of what is distinctive in learning to speak (Wittgenstein contrasted it with learning a foreign language) and with the wonder of coming to have something to say. For Skinner, learning anything — to speak, to think, to somersault — is acquiring certain techniques. In *Walden Two*, speaking about education, Frazier says, 'We don't need to teach "subjects" at all. We teach only the techniques of learning and thinking.' These words echo those of Gorgias.

For Skinner, just as all education is 'behavioural engineering', all human interaction consists of mutual control. It is significant that he speaks of institutions as 'agencies'. Thus schools are educational agencies. They are not there to educate the child, but to carry out certain educational policies. In *Science and Human Behaviour* he speaks of 'the behaviour resulting from educational control'. In fact, like Gorgias, Skinner sees no distinction between teaching and manipulation. He writes in *Beyond Freedom and Dignity*: 'It is a surprising fact that those who object most violently to the manipulation of behaviour nevertheless make the most vigorous efforts to manipulate minds' (p. 92). What he calls 'manipulation of minds' is what we would call 'the teaching of new ideas', just as what we refer to as 'thinking' and 'deciding' are, for Skinner, forms of 'self-manipulation'. The educational institution, he says, teaches the student to *think*. 'It establishes a special repertoire which has as its effect the manipulation of variables which encourage the appearance of solutions to problems' (*SHB*, p. 411). It does not occur to him to ask what counts as a solution to a problem and how we evaluate the search for solutions. A *choice* too for Skinner is the manipulation, by the agent, of 'some of the variables of which his behaviour is a function' (ibid., p. 242). We have already noted the paradox in this account.

In fact, all *doings* are analysed by Skinner as the application of techniques by the agent. He is not aware of the vicious regress in this analysis owing to the fact that the application of a technique is

itself an action. But for Skinner, in the last analysis, there is no distinction between doing something and something happening to
one, between voluntary and involuntary movement, between
reason and causes.

I said that for Skinner, all human relationship and interaction is
manipulation and mutual control: 'The girl who wants another
date must be sure that her friend's behaviour in inviting her and in
keeping the appointment is suitably reinforced' (*SHB*, p. 74).
Indeed, Skinner's whole perspective is 'conditioned' by his
association with animals in the artificial setting of his experiments.
The girl who wants to see her boyfriend and to be with him is
described as 'wanting another date', on the analogy of the pigeon
who wants more food, a greater ration of grains. And although
sometimes what the girl wants comes to little more than this, at
other times it would be a travesty to suggest that it is. But Skinner
cannot see more than this in the girl's relationship with her boyfriend. It is analysed into discrete packages — dates, kisses, smiles,
touches — until the whole relationship is reduced to a series of
mutual feeding. For the feeding to continue the feeder must be
reinforced; thus the pigeon stretches its neck higher and higher.
What a pathetic view of courtship!

We have already seen that Skinner sees no real distinction
between someone who likes or is fond of a friend and someone who
associates with a 'friend' for what he gets out of him. In fact, for
Skinner, affection is a 'generalised reinforcer': 'It may be
especially connected with sexual contact as a primary reinforcer'
(ibid., p. 78). It is apparently something which parents *use* in
shaping their children's behaviour: 'We use this generalised
reinforcer to establish and shape the behaviour of others, particularly in education' (ibid.). Incidentally, the child's parents here are
listed under 'educational agencies', and what they do in the
upbringing of their children is referred to as 'their techniques of
control'. I ask again whether giving affection is controlling the
behaviour of another person. It is so only in the special case where
a person threatens to withdraw his love or affection. But then,
when love and affection can be turned on and off like a tap, they no
longer are what they pretend to be. For Skinner, however, even
asking someone to do something or thanking him is manipulating
his behaviour. In fact, he classifies thanking with bribery (*SHB*,
p. 317).

For Skinner, ethics and religion, like education, are also forms
of control and manipulation. The pigeon stretches its neck higher

and higher because each time it does so it receives food. This is a 'contingency of reinforcement' artificially provided by the experimenter. There are many such consequences of a person's behaviour provided by nature which are reinforcing. In general, however, they are arranged by the community with a view to encouraging certain forms of behaviour and restraining others. This, Skinner says, is the whole point of ethical training (*SHB*, p. 240). Note that what is in question is described by Skinner as 'training'. He does not and cannot take account of the difference which moral learning makes to our understanding and conception of life. And so he can see no distinction between doing something because one believes it to be right and doing it simply because one has been brought up to do it — a distinction insisted on by all great writers in ethics. Nor, as we have already seen, can he distinguish between doing something because one believes it to be right and doing it for a reward or out of a fear of punishment.

We have seen that Skinner equates 'good' with 'rewarding', though he prefers to talk of 'positive reinforcement'. He assimilates judgements of absolute value to conditional judgements of value. 'You *ought* to take an umbrella' means, he says, 'You will be reinforced by taking an umbrella.' Likewise, 'You *ought* to love your neighbour' means 'Loving your fellow men is approved by the group of which you are a member, and the approval of your fellow men is positively reinforcing you' (*SHB*, p. 429). 'You *ought* to tell the truth' means 'If you are reinforced by the approval of your fellow men, you will be reinforced when you tell the truth.' 'You *ought* not to steal' means 'If you tend to avoid punishment, avoid stealing' (*BFD*, pp. 112–14). He adds that these judgements are no more normative than 'If coffee keeps you awake when you want to go to sleep, don't drink it.' He says explicitly that moral behaviour 'depends upon the control exerted by the social environment' (ibid., p. 110). 'A man . . . behaves bravely when environmental circumstances induce him to do so' (ibid., p. 192), for instance, if he is afraid to be shamed for behaving in a cowardly way. Plato argues that such a man is not really brave.

In short, Skinner's view is that moral actions are the result of manipulation, and that moral judgements are instruments of manipulation, although those who make them are also victims of manipulation: 'We blame in order to control someone's future behaviour' (*SHB*, p. 351). Compare Frazier's distinction between benevolent and oppressive control with Gorgias's distinction between persuasion and force.

What Skinner has to say about religion is equally shallow. He thinks of Christian virtues as 'techniques of self-control' (1976, p. 97). Christian precepts are policies. For instance, 'Loving our enemies' is a technique for avoiding the ravages of hatred (*SHB*, p. 240). 'Turning the other cheek' is a technique for satiating an aggressor by submitting to him (ibid., p. 319). In *Walden Two* Frazier rather condescendingly gives Jesus credit for having stumbled upon the advantage of positive reinforcement over punishment:

> We've all seen countless instances of the temporary effect of force, but clear evidence of the effect of not using force is rare. That's why I insist that Jesus, who was apparently the first to discover the power of refusing to punish, must have hit upon the principle by accident. He certainly had none of the experimental evidence which is available to us today, and I can't conceive that it was possible, no matter what the man's genius, to have discovered the principle from casual observation.
>
> Jesus discovered one principle because it had immediate consequences, and he got another thrown in for good measure.
>
> To 'do good to those who despitefully use you' has two unrelated consequences. You gain the peace of mind we talked about the other day. Let the stronger man push you around — at least you avoid the torture of your own rage. *That's* the immediate consequence. What an astonishing discovery it must have been to find that in the long run you could *control the stronger man* in the same way!' (pp. 245–6; see also p. 97)

We have already seen that for Skinner the hermit is no different from the hippie and the hobo. As for the Christian conception of 'an all-seeing God', Skinner speaks of such a god as 'a super-spy', 'a sneaking supervisor'. He says that it 'makes escape from the punisher practically impossible, and punitive contingencies are then maximally effective. People behave well although there is no visible supervisor' (*BFD*, p. 70). In *Walden Two* Skinner's spokesman, Frazier, argues that given the scientific organisation of society, along the lines laid down by behavioural engineering, there is no need for such a god, or any other kind of god: 'Religious faith becomes irrelevant when the fears which nourish it

are allayed and the hopes fulfilled here on earth' (p. 185).
Reference to another world is clearly illusory for Skinner, as it was
for Freud too: 'Hope for a better world in the future? We like it
well enough here on earth. We don't ask to be consoled for a vale
of tears by promises of heaven' (p. 186). Clearly, Skinner, along
with many others, cannot see an alternative conception of all such
references to spiritual matters. (For an alternative conception see
Simone Weil (1950), *La Connaissance Surnaturelle*, especially what
she says about the corrupting effect of the need for consolation and
compensation in the spiritual life.)

All theology is rejected in the community of *Walden Two*. Nevertheless, Frazier adds, 'the practices of organised religion' have
been retained or 'borrowed': 'to inspire group loyalty and
strengthen the observance of the Code' (p. 185). He mentions
regular Sunday meetings where 'a philosophical, poetic, or
religious work is read or acted out'.

> We like the effect of this upon the speech of the community. It
> gives us a common stock of literary allusions. Then there's a
> brief 'lesson' — of the utmost importance in maintaining an
> observance of the Code. Usually items are chosen for dis-
> cussion which deal with self-control and certain kinds of social
> articulation. (p. 185)

Finally, he mentions the music, which he says 'serves the same
purpose as in a church — it makes the service enjoyable and establishes a mood. The weekly lesson is a sort of group therapy. And it
seems to be all we need' (pp. 185–6).

Just think of Bach writing mood music for the churches, and ask
if his music could have been what it is. Imagine reading works of
philosophy and literature to acquire a common stock of literary
allusions. Finally, think of engaging in religious practices as a form
of therapy. You will get an inkling of the degraded and shallow
conception of the human spirit that is characteristic of our age.
Skinner is no more than its mouthpiece.

8

Skinner's Conception of
'the Good Life'

Not surprisingly, Skinner's own values are as shallow as his analysis of moral values and religious precepts. He believes that 'the good life' can be planned and realised by means of 'cultural and behavioural engineering'. For he holds that man is a lump of clay that can be moulded by operant conditioning: 'Operant conditioning shapes behaviour as a sculptor shapes a lump of clay' (*SHB*, p. 91).

The good life, the ideal world, for Skinner, is one where conflict between people is at a minimum, where people are efficient and happy, where they are free from what Skinner calls 'unproductive emotions' (1976, pp. 92–3). These are emotions which 'interfere with the effective behaviour of the individual' (*SHB*, p. 191) — such emotions as fear, anxiety, guilt, envy, jealousy. It is a society where people are made to co-operate by means of positive reinforcement and not the fear of punishment. It is comfortable and safe. It is a world in which 'behaviour likely to be punished seldom or never occurs' (*BFD*, pp. 68–9). Skinner adds, 'We try to design such a world for those who cannot solve the problem of punishment for themselves, such as babies, retardates, or psychotics, and if it could be done for everyone, much time and energy would be saved (ibid.).

In other words, it is a world so arranged that the risks of people hurting themselves or each other are reduced to a minimum, where they are taken care of, not allowed to make a mess of their lives. It is a world in which responsibility is reduced to a minimum; where people are not blamed, not punished. As Frazier puts it, 'A moral or ethical lapse, whether in explicit violation of the Code or not, needs treatment, not punishment' (1976, p. 159).

It is a world in which envy, jealousy, possessiveness, hatred, guilt and remorse have been reduced to a minimum, but so has gratitude, as expressed in thanking (ibid., p. 92), and where wonder has been replaced by curiosity. It is a world from which the need for moral reflection and moral struggle has been eliminated, a world which 'builds only automatic goodness', a system 'so perfect that no one will need to be good' (*BFD*, p. 69).

Frazier certainly believes that what makes for evil is the product of the environment and can, therefore, be eradicated:

> As for emotions — we aren't free of them all, nor should we like to be. But the meaner and more annoying — the emotions which breed unhappiness — are almost unknown here, like unhappiness itself. We don't need them any longer in our struggle for existence, and it's easier . . . and pleasanter to dispense with them . . . We arrange them [things] otherwise here . . . Sorrow and hate — and the high-voltage excitements of anger, fear, and rage — are out of proportion with the needs of modern life, and they're wasteful and dangerous . . . In a co-operative society there's no jealousy because there's no need for jealousy. (1976, pp. 92–3)

There are serious considerations, however, which should make one doubtful whether such surgery, through environmental manipulation, if it were possible at all, would leave people otherwise just as they were — capable of reaching heights in their spirituality and depth in their compassion and love. A love, for instance, that is incapable of grieving its object's loss, of feeling sorrow when its object is harmed, of feeling jealousy when the beloved gives his or her affection to someone else. Is such a love capable of reaching the depth portrayed in our literature? Is a person in whose life there is no logical room for guilt and remorse capable of the kind of good deed that is an object of wonder for us? Indeed, Frazier himself admits that the only kind of goodness for which there is a place in his ideal world is 'automatic goodness'. We may wonder, as Frazier does not, what is so good about such 'goodness' — a question I would not expect Skinner to understand.

So, in Skinner's view, there is no insoluble problem of evil, no social evils that cannot be done away with:

> The real issue is the effectiveness of techniques of control. We shall not solve the problems of alcoholism and juvenile

delinquency by increasing a sense of responsibility. It is the environment which is 'responsible' for the objectionable behaviour, and it is the environment, not some attribute of the individual, which must be changed (*BFD*, pp. 76–7).

Given such a conception of the problem of evil, punishment becomes simply a method of control, to be evaluated in terms of its consequence and 'by-products': 'It reduces the overall efficiency and happiness of the group' (*SHB*, p. 190).

Frazier boasts, 'We've done all we can to avoid unhappiness' (p. 130). This is obviously one of the touchstones of his conception of the good life. His critic, the philosopher Castle, complains, not with great force:

> So far as I can see, you've blocked every path through which man was to struggle upward toward salvation. Intelligence, initiative — you have filled their places with a sort of degraded instinct, engineered compulsion. Walden Two is a marvel of efficient co-ordination — as efficient as an ant-hill. (p. 237)

Dostoyevsky has parodied such a utopia in Ivan's legend of 'The Grand Inquisitor' (1957) and criticised the conception of man at the centre of it. The society at the head of which the Grand Inquisitor presides is a veritable 'ant-heap' modelled on the idea of the socialist radicals and progressives of Dostoyevsky's times. The Grand Inquisitor's conception of human happiness is as shallow as the one which informs Frazier in his blueprint of Walden Two. He, like Frazier, has a low opinion of men; he believes in manipulating them for what he thinks of as their good. Like Frazier he believes in the illusion of freedom for men: 'People today are more persuaded than ever that they have perfect freedom . . . Men would rather have bread than freedom.' In other words, they would rather have food, clothes, warmth, have their lives arranged for them so that they can have comfort and harmony, than think things out for themselves and face the consequences of their choices and decisions. 'Men want to find someone to whom they can hand over their freedom. Only one who can appease their conscience can take over their freedom.' He points out that Jesus refused to do so. Jesus, he says, has laid upon men so many cares and unanswerable problems. And he, the Grand Inquisitor, boasts, like Frazier, of having taken these away from men and made them happy.

The big difference between the Grand Inquisitor and Frazier is that the former knows the higher things he has foregone for the sake of a 'childlike happiness' for men, knows what it means to be free and to bear responsibility for one's actions:

> And all will be happy, all the millions of creatures, except the hundred thousand who rule over them. For only we, who guard the mystery, shall be unhappy. There will be thousands of millions of happy babes, and a hundred thousand sufferers who have taken upon themselves the curse of the knowledge of good and evil.

Whereas in Skinner's conception of psychology and in Walden Two, a community portrayed as running itself, like an automaton, a recognition of all this is nonexistent.

9

Punishment and Behavioural Therapy

I want to point out very briefly the consequences of Skinner's behaviourism for his concepts of punishment and psychotherapy.

I take these two together because Skinner regards them as forms of behaviour correction, of control of unwelcome behaviour. He regards the behaviour to be corrected as simply what the person in question has *learned* by means of operant conditioning. The kind of questions about motives which we might raise in both connections have no place within Skinner's conceptual framework and are, therefore, treated as irrelevant to the notions of punishment and psychotherapy. As for the reasons for regarding certain forms of behaviour as 'needing correction', Skinner thinks of them as purely utilitarian in character and, ultimarely, not as reasons at all, but the consequences of Darwinian survival working through the societies to which people belong.

Skinner does not really see any difference between punishment and psychotherapy except in terms of effectiveness of control, and the additional side-effects of the former, judged in the same terms as the behaviour to be controlled is judged originally. On these grounds, Skinner rejects punishment as undesirable and he recommends treatment or psychotherapy instead, which means behavioural therapy. In fact, he believes that behavioural engineering would eliminate the need for either, a form of engineering in which he sees no place for punishment if its objectives are to be successfully achieved. Skinner considers punishment to be an outmoded form of behavioural control — outmoded because 'in the long run punishment does not eliminate the behaviour punished' (*SHB*, p. 190). After a time 'the conditioned negative reinforcer undergoes extinction . . . and the punished behaviour eventually emerges' (ibid., p. 189). Futhermore, 'the technique of punishment has unfortunate by-products . . . The aversive stimuli which are needed generate emotions, including predispositions to escape or retaliate, and disabling anxieties' (ibid., pp. 182–3). These by-products are 'unfortunate' in that they 'interfere with the effective behaviour of the individual' and prevent his co-operation with others.

I repeat: for Skinner, punishment is something that *can* be replaced by psychotherapeutic treatment (conceptual claim) and, indeed *ought* to be (normative claim). There is no conceptual difference between punishment and therapy; both are methods of 'behaviour correction'. The only difference is to be found in how well they work. Of course, what Skinner means by 'punishment' is not the same as what we mean by it. Not having succeeded in purging his own thoughts of their 'traditional' encroachment, he sometimes gives the impression of regarding punishment not merely as undesirable, for the reasons I have indicated, but also as pointless, since to punish someone presupposes that one regards him as responsible for what he has done. In *Science and Human Behaviour* he points out that the category of people 'we no longer blame' and exonerate from punishment is getting wider. 'The insane have long since been cleared of responsibility for their condition, and the kinds of neurotic or psychotic behaviour to which we now apply this extenuation are multiplying' (p. 8). The two points are different and do not apply to the same concept of punishment. It is punishment in Skinner's sense of 'behaviour correction' that is 'ineffective' and punishment in what Skinner regards as the traditional sense that is 'inappropriate'. But Skinner does not always hold this distinction clearly in view.

It is true that when one punishes someone or wants him to be punished by the appropriate authorities, one regards him as responsible for what he has done; and Skinner does reject the possibility of responsible action while retaining the notion of punishment. It is this notion which he employs when he says that in the long run, punishment cannot succeed in its objective. I want to note that Skinner's conception of the aim or objective of punishment is both narrow and shallow, and that this is because he employs an attenuated conception of punishment. Punishment, for him, is simply the correction of unwelcome behaviour by aversive means. We have seen in what sense he regards the behaviour to be corrected as unwelcome. It is unwelcome for Skinner either in the sense that it happens to he disapproved of by the society in question, or in the sense that it does not suit the punishing 'agency', or Skinner himself on the basis of his own 'enlightened' criteria. However, he does not think of these criteria as normative. (See his analysis of 'ought' in *BFD*, p. 114.)

Skinner cannot take into account the fact that punishment is a response to a wrong, seen as deserving punishment, and that as such, it embodies a judgement of value. All this is archaic from Skinner's 'enlightened' point of view. As for our distinction, in part already eroded, between 'correction and behaviour' and 'moral or spiritual change', it is not something which Skinner's behaviourism can accommodate. I doubt whether he even understands it. He hardly understands what it is to change one's mind.

Skinner's concept of psychotherapy as 'behavioural therapy' suffers from similar defects as his concept of punishment. Behind his concept of punishment is his conception of crime as simply learned behaviour which needs correction and of evil as a product of the environment. Behind his idea of therapy lies his conception of what the person to be treated suffers from as the product of 'maladaptive learning'. Just as in connection with punishment he could not accommodate any distinction between change of behaviour and change of soul, so in connection with therapy he cannot allow any distinction between 'behaviour modification' and 'self-transformation'.

It may well be possible in some cases to modify a person's behaviour by 'behavioural therapy', and consequently to spare him the specific troubles which the behaviour in question got him into, *without* in any way helping him resolve or come to terms with the inner conflicts from which that behaviour springs. It is true that not all such behaviour may spring from inner conflicts. On the other hand, there is no denying that *some* of it does. I would not expect a follower of Skinner to be sensitive to the 'inner dimension' of the troubles for which people seek psychotherapeutic help. Indeed, behavioural therapy does not (and given its conceptual framework, cannot) offer any scope for the healing of splits within the person, nor for his emotional development towards greater autonomy.

What it offers may be just what a person needs in some cases, and it may well work in such cases. But my own suspicion is that such cases form a relatively small class in the spectrum of people seeking therapeutic help.

I do not myself know how such a spectrum is to be delineated. I can only say that I do not think there is *one* set of criteria (e.g.

medical) that will do the work. It is, I believe, important to have a lively awareness of the variety in the cases that fall within it, of their interrelations, and of their relations to those that are relatively peripheral and even remain on the outside. There are many difficult questions here which I cannot see Skinner discussing. But one thing is clear to me, namely that the notion of 'maladaptation' used in behavioural therapy will not take us very far.

10

Science and Human Behaviour

1. Scientific generalisation and the individual person

In *Beyond Freedom and Dignity* Skinner writes:

> Physics and biology have come a long way, but there has been no comparable development of anything like a science of human behaviour. Greek physics and biology are now of historical interest only . . . but the dialogues of Plato are still assigned to students and cited as if they threw light on human behaviour. Aristotle could not have understood a page of modern physics or biology, but Socrates and his friends would have little trouble in following most current discussions of human affairs. (p. 11)

He goes on to say that the reason for this is not that the early Greeks 'knew all there was to know about human behaviour'. For what they knew did not amount to much. Rather, his explanation of why the dialogues of Plato are still assigned to students is that we do not have anything better (p. 12). We have nothing better because we have reduplicated in our thinking the 'fatal flaw' to be found in early Greek thinking about human behaviour. Thus, Skinner argues, 'whereas Greek physics and biology . . . led eventually to modern science, Greek theories of human behaviour led nowhere'.

If we have nothing better, this is not because we have made no progress in this field. Skinner's very idea of linear progress here is one that needs criticism. If we have nothing better, this is because Plato represents one of the peaks of human thought on human nature. There have, of course, been other peaks. Furthermore, Skinner misunderstands the relation between philosophy and psychology. He thinks of philosophy as the pre-scientific stage of psychology. He believes that those methods which have proved their worth in the physical sciences are applicable in psychology. When they are applied, speculation will be replaced by precise and testable results. This, in turn, will make it possible for psychologists to deal more efficiently with the problems of maladjustment, difficulties in learning at school, unhappiness in human relationships in the context of the family, courtship, work and so on. *Walden Two* is a literary representation of the realisation of this ideal.

This view of scientific psychology and the character of human problems is not confined to behaviourism. It is shared by a wide circle of contemporary academic psychologists. (Thus see George A. Miller (1979), for instance, in *Psychology*, Ch. 1, 'Psychology, Science and Man'.)

What is interesting and needs criticism is the way Skinner and others dismiss what is not experimental as 'speculation', and the way they tie up observation with experimental method. The 'fatal flaw' which Skinner attributes to Socrates' way of thinking about human behaviour is that it is in terms of concepts which prevent his observations from finding expression in scientifically testable statements. So we have two ideas here, related as the two sides of the same coin: (1) That a scientific psychology replaces speculation with testable results, and (2) that the problems to which these results are applicable are soluble, since they are themselves the product of ignorance and prejudice. Thus the misery that has plagued human beings until the present is avoidable. This is quite explicitly stated by Frazier in *Walden Two*.

In his book *The Danger of Words*, Drury argues that such a view disregards the reality of evil as a positive force in human life. Hatred, pride, greed, envy, callousness and the diverse ways in which they work in human affairs in opposition to love, compassion, forgiveness, gratitude and generosity, are part of the very tissue of human life. A psychology which ignores this becomes shallow. I pointed out earlier that it is an illusion to suppose, as Skinner does, that you can remove the first half of these things without changing the character of what you leave, without castrating the power for good in human life and the capacity for depth of experience. Drury argues that if we can see that many of these problems are not soluble, we can free ourselves of the shallow optimism engendered by the *pretensions* of science. We may then find a different way of meeting them.

I will not pursue this question now, but would like to return to the first of the two ideas above: Are the questions which psychology researches into amenable to experimental study? I do not wish to deny that *some* are. But I would deny that psychology is *confined* to such questions. I agree with Wittgenstein that a psychology which confines itself to them is 'barren'. For it steers clear of the questions we are most interested in as human beings. I also agree that one who holds that psychology is a 'young science' whose questions, not at present amenable to experimental study, will one day become subject to such a study, is 'confused' (Wittgenstein, 1963, Pt. II, Sec. xiv). Drury (1973, p. 43) says that such a psychology shows 'a thoughtless attitude to the deeper problems of life'.

What reason is there for thinking that there are many psychological questions which are not amenable to experimental investigation? There are many reasons. One of these is bound up with the fact that human beings possess tha capacity to talk and live a life which would not be what it is without language. Its concepts enter the thoughts and actions of those that participate in such a life. To understand people's actions and responses you have to understand the concepts that enter into these. Psychological explanations must, therefore, incorporate these concepts in one way or another. There is nothing comparable to this in the physical sciences. This is the main theme developed by Winch (1958).

Connected with this is the fact that we come to know a person largely by talking with him, eliciting a response from him in what we say, ask or do; a response to which we ourselves respond. The person to whom we talk can lie to us, not be frank with us, hide his thoughts and feelings. So if we are to know him we must have his consent; we have to make contact with him. What is in question is very different from observing something, if we take observing a culture under the microscope or an animal through a one-way screen as our paradigm. The kind of observation of another human being that leads to knowledge of him as an individual is part of our interaction with him. In the course of such interaction he tells us things, and he may hide behind words. We have to understand his language and also come to know what to make of his words, what weight to attach to them. The observation in question is not characterised by the kind of detachment that belongs to scientific observation and inductive knowledge.

Indeed, the kind of knowledge of human beings which informs our interest in and responses to an individual person is not inductive in character. It is not arrived at by means of generalisations; its generality is not that which characterises a scientific theory. Wittgenstein says that 'some' can learn this knowledge: 'Not, however, by taking a course in it, but through "experience"' (1963, p. 227). The experience in question is acquired in active participation in activities with other people, coming into contact with them in the pursuit of joint interests, or in the course of struggles over conflicting interests. It is not acquired in a 'wait and see' manner following active intervention. It is not the fruit of detached curiosity, but of active interest. It is not the result of theoretical interest, an interest in questions, but of an interest in people. It is often mediated by reflection on the individual and his circumstances, as well as on men and their diverse ways — such reflection as we find in literature.

What we learn in a particular case, from contact with an individual, makes a difference to what we see in another case, to what we are able to bring to our contact with another person. It may also enable us to make general remarks. But the *generality* in question is not that of a generalisation. This is connected with the fact that we are not interested in people as types, or as members of a class, but as *individuals* — or at least normally we are. This is what makes people so different from things, things which we normally grasp in terms of their general characteristics or common properties. In rare cases these drop into the background and we see a thing as an individual, or paint a scene in such a way that what we produce is not a picture postcard. It captures the scene in its individual uniqueness. This is how the artist is interested in things. It is the antithesis of the way the scientist is interested in them. There is here some analogy to the way we are interested in people; but the analogy is limited.

It is not easy to say what it comes to. But one thing is clear, namely that if it were possible to put such an interest aside completely one would no longer see people as people. Skinner, as a scientific psychologist, is interested in people not as people, but as 'organisms'. Within the framework of his psychology there is no place for most of the questions we ask about ourselves. This is a loss which Skinner makes light of and to which I shall return in the following section. A more serious criticism is that Skinner's 'scientific' interest in people is not rooted in anything real, in the way that our scientific interest in things is. The latter is rooted in our interest in things as objects we can manipulate and in their effects as phenomena we wish to be able to anticipate. Whereas Skinner's interest in people as 'objects of manipulation' and in their behaviour as 'phenomena to be controlled and predicted' is largely the product of conceptual confusion. Insofar as it is real it is a corrupt interest, the fruit of an uprooted culture.

Another reason why the most interesting questions of psychology are not amenable to experimental investigation is this. An experiment is something one can repeat. The environment in which an experiment is repeated is tightly controlled; it must remain the same if it is to be possible to compare the results. What is included in or excluded from this environment makes a causal difference to the result obtained; but it does not affect how the result is to be characterised. The same result is conceivable in different circumstances even if, as a matter of fact, it proves unobtainable. With what psychology is interested in it is mostly otherwise. The remark that a man utters, for instance, will have a different significance in different circumstances; in different surroundings the same gesture, movement, or even action will manifest very different feelings, qualities of mind and character. Here we have a serious logical limit to experimentation in psychology.

I have just mentioned the way the identity of what is in question logically depends on its surroundings. This is true of a great deal of what interests us in people. Thus given the restricted conditions necessary for experimental investigation and one has excluded much of this. That is why an experimental psychology is bound to be 'barren'. On the other side of the coin, most of the states and qualities that are relevant to what interests us in people have diverse manifestations. Any one of the words we use to refer to or describe qualities and capacities of mind and character in people covers 'many manifestations of life', and the phenomena which constitute these manifestations are 'widely scattered' (Wittgenstein, 1967, sec. 110). There is nothing to be abstracted from them all, whether it be the diverse manifestations of love or intelligence, such that we can say 'this is its *essential* nature'. This point is connected with my remark on the kind of generality there is in our knowledge of mankind. If we abstract or construct such an 'essence' or general character in the name of science we shall leave out much that is of vital interest to us. This is one reason why there can be no unified theory e.g. of love or learning and why their presentation belongs to literature rather than science.

So the emotions, feelings, states of mind and qualities of

character, about which one would expect psychology to have something to say, cannot be abstracted for scientific treatment from their surroundings in the individual's life. But in any case many of these manifestations are subject to the individual's will and so they may be used by him to hide his feelings, to disguise his intentions. It is the fact that he speaks a language and can tell us things about himself that is of primary importance here. It does not seem to me that experimental psychologists have sufficiently pondered on the significance of this fact.

Furthermore, what an individual feels or desires is not *his* in the sense that the properties of a thing are *its* properties. They do not 'define' him, give him the identity he has, in the way that the latter determine a thing's identity. A thing's identity is its membership of overlapping classes. The identity of a human being as an individual is a matter of what he makes of himself in a sense that needs discussion.

This is by no means incompatible with the fact that man is a social creature. We find our individuality in the life we share with others. There is certainly an important sense in which what one can make of oneself is made possible and given limits by the language and culture of the society to which one belongs. But 'making something of oneself' is the operative expression here and it is the antithesis of mere conformity. To the extent to which we conform we are one of many, not individuals. We copy and so reflect what is outside us, and it makes us what we are. In contrast, to the extent to which we make it our own or turn away from it we become what we make of ourselves. But it is what we learn from others in our interaction with them in the course of common activities, in the surroundings of a common life and culture, that makes it possible for us to respond in these ways, to endorse or repudiate, to accept or rebel. It is the social character of our life, the fact that we are members of a community, share a common life and understanding with others, and think in terms of concepts they understand, that makes for the possibility of a *dimension of the personal* in human life. There is nothing paradoxical in this claim.

The French philosopher Sartre has given much thought to this sense in which a man differs from a thing. A thing, he argued, is 'defined' by the properties or attributes it possesses. The hardness, colour, shape and chemical properties of this stone inviduate it, they make it the particular stone it is. We identify it by means of them. An individual human being, on the other hand, 'transcends' his feelings, desires, and the various features of his character. He does so in the sense that he can himself be aware of them and so endorse or repudiate them, thus assuming responsibility for what he is. They do not belong to him in the sense that the properties of the stone belong to it. Thus (1) where a man repudiates an aspect of his character, say his greed, there is an obvious sense in which he transcends it. He does not act from greed, at least he tries not to, and when he gives in he feels ashamed. (2) Where he endorses it too he transcends it in a perhaps less obvious sense. He says, 'Each man has but one life and I say that while you are alive grab what you can so long as you can keep independent.' We can say that he has made the greed his own; it is not something just *given*. (3) It would be *that* if he gave no thought to it, if it did not figure in his consciousness, if he acquiesced in it passively. In this third case he is greedy in the mode of a greedy puppy, he has sunk into a thing-like existence. Even then he is not really a thing, of course. He *can* act with thought and he can be behind what he does. So we can hold him responsible for having failed to act with thought and conviction.

These three possibilities exhaust the field, and in none of them is the person identical with his greed. Sartre sometimes puts this by saying that 'there is no such thing as human nature, but only a human condition'. This is the reverse of what Skinner would mean if he spoke these words. I am thinking of his 'environmentalism'. What Sartre means is that the nature or character we attribute to a person, whatever its source, is part of the condition which he has to take into account when taking decisions and acting. When it does 'define' him, as in the case of his deepest moral convictions, it is he who makes it his own, not *it* that makes him what he is.

Sartre also speaks of freedom in this connection: 'There is no difference between the being of man and his *being-free*.' It is important to notice that freedom here is something which is claimed to characterise human existence as such, and not something which distinguishes between one kind of life or action and another. Therefore the attribution of freedom to people in this sense does not rule out the possibility of the loss of freedom within the realm so characterised. Sartre's claim that 'man is condemned to be free' is thus primarily a *philosophical* assertion. It can be compared to the philosophical assertion that 'man has a soul', which in no way implies that men cannot lose their soul.

To return to the dichotomy between observation and speculation. Of course observation is central to psychological knowledge. What I am critical of is the way it is used in the context of experiments. I mean the kind of inductive role assigned to it, the kind of prediction and generalisation it is made to licence, the narrow focus it is made to serve at the expense of what surrounds the point of focus, the level of generality at which it concentrates on its object, the way it attempts to grasp it from 'outside'. 'Outside' here is to be contrasted with the point of view internal to what is observed, the point of view which enters into and in that sense 'defines' the identity of the response or behaviour observed.

Observation, however, can assume a different focus. It can look at the individual from *within*, in the way that a dramatist pictures his behaviour and responses, that is, as directed to a situation as the person himself sees it. A picture of the significance of the situation for the individual is built from the details of his behaviour, his facial expressions, his comments and the surrounding reactions. What is thus depicted enables us to see the situation through *his* eyes. This, in turn, enriches what we observe in the behaviour depicted. Such a focus is historical rather than inductive. The question 'What led up to it?' is not directed at formulating hypotheses about repeatable causal sequences. It seeks to gather an individual story which helps us to make better sense of what we see.

What I am getting at it is that the ideals of experimental psychology are not the only scientific ones, in a broad sense of that term, and that if psychology is primarily concerned with the study of human beings it is first and foremost a *clinical* subject. What I mean to emphasise is not its kinship to medicine, but the importance of the detailed study of concrete cases in their particular setting. This is almost the exact opposite of the experimental method which is orientated towards the abstract and general, and towards repeatable characteristics, and away from the particular circumstances which surround these. The circumstances in question are, of course, those of human life, and the possibility of their sense comes from the society to which people belong.

2. Complexity and conceptual incommensurability

Skinner nearly admits that an experimental psychology bypasses the questions we are most interested in as human beings. But he then dismisses these questions: 'The dramatic things in human behaviour are tied up with our everyday experience with people. Accounts of this experience [however] are cast in a dualism that has become part of our language' ('Behaviourism at Fifty', p. 100).

The implication is that these 'dramatic things' are no more than the shadows of an inappropriate conceptual scheme. In the same paper he admits that 'no scientific analysis of behaviour will be as rich as *The Brothers Karamazov*'. But then he adds, 'nor will the physicist's analysis of the world be as rich as walking around the campus. They are "not there to be rich" ' (p. 104). He says something similar in *Science and Human Behaviour*: 'The "case history" has a richness and flavour which are in decided contrast with general principles' (p. 18).

He then goes on to argue that just as in physics there are not two worlds, the world of common sense and that of theoretical physics, so in psychology there are not two worlds, the world of purpose and intention and that of scientific psychology. Once we are clear about what can be deduced in a particular case from the abstract theoretical descriptions, we shall stop worrying about what has been lost:

> What the science of physics has to say about the world is dull and colourless to the beginning student when compared with his daily experience, but he later discovers that it is actually a more incisive account of even the single instance. When we wish to deal effectively with the single instance, we turn to science for help. (ibid.)

One question here concerns the relation between the language of primary, measurable qualities in which theoretical physics is conducted, and the language of 'secondary qualities', such as colour, which Goethe complained is left out of physics. If our calculations enable us to deduce the wavelengths of the light emitted from certain particles, we can predict what colours we shall be able to see. In the same way, Skinner believes, from the elements ('acts') that are strengthened whenever they occur we are able to predict the probability of all responses containing the same elements. The element is the 'behavioural atom' which may never appear by itself, but it is 'the essential ingredient or component of all observed instances' (*SHB*, p. 94).

We may well be able to say that when certain measurements are carried out and certain results obtained, the light measured will be seen by the normal human eye to have such-and-such colours. In contrast, I have suggested that from no description of movements that take place, however detected, can we infer what a person is *doing* — what he is up to or engaged in, what he is responding to and in what way. The deductive relations which may hold in the physical sciences do not hold in psychology. We have seen why not.

'When we wish to deal effectively with the single instance we turn to science for help.' By 'deal effectively' Skinner means 'predict and control'. I have suggested that this is something which Skinner imports into psychology and that it does not really belong with the kind of interest we take in human beings.

Skinner clearly thinks that what we are interested in is simply a *complex* form of that in terms of which he formulates his theories. Hence the passage he quotes from Tolstoy's *War and Peace*:

> No single disease can be fully understood in a living person; for every living person has his individual peculiarities and always has his own peculiar, new, complex complaints unknown to medicine — not a disease of the lungs, of the kidneys, of the skin, of the heart, and so on, as described in medical books, but a disease that consists of one out of the innumerable combinations of ailments of those organs. (*SHB*, pp. 18–19)

Skinner's argument is: If you cannot rule out the possibility of a science of medicine on the grounds advanced by Tolstoy, why should you expect to rule out the possibility of a science of behaviour? I have argued that human behaviour, as we conceive it, has logical peculiarities which you do not have in the case of the function of our organs.

In any case, I suspect that Tolstoy did not make clear, in the passage quoted, what he meant. He was getting at something quite different from what Skinner makes of it, namely how little medical knowledge can help us understand Natasha's *malaise* or *state of soul*. If so, then the quotation from Tolstoy is likely to backfire on Skinner. For, indeed, however much the state of Natasha's internal organs may have contributed to her *malaise*, they could not possibly explain it.

Skinner says, 'Tolstoy was justified in calling every sickness a unique event. Every action of the individual is unique, as well as every event in physics and chemistry' (ibid., p. 19). But this is a misunderstanding of the sense in which a person is an individual and as such unique. In Skinner's sense what has no second instantiation is unique. In this sense I doubt that every sickness is a unique event. Be that as it may, the sense in which a person is an individual, and in that sense unique, is not that there is no one else quite *like him*, but that no one else, however much like him, is *him*. When we speak of a person having *made his own* moral beliefs shared by thousands of others, it is the latter sense of uniqueness that is in question.

Skinner falls into the same confusion when discussing 'the unity of a self'. He runs together 'self', 'personality' and 'character' (see *SHB*, p. 285). But while my character is unique only if it is qualitatively different from anybody else's character, what makes me unique as a person is that nobody else can take my decisions, fulfil my obligations, love or die in my place. He cannot decide in my place, for what he decides is no good to me unless it comes from me.

Skinner writes:

In a scientific analysis it is seldom possible to proceed directly to complex cases. We begin with the simple and build up to the complex, step by step. In its early years any science is vulnerable to the charge that it neglects important instances. Boyle's Law, relating the volume of a gas to its pressure, was a significant advance in knowledge, but a contemporary critic could easily have denounced it as a flagrant oversimplification . . .

In a science of behaviour we begin in the simplest way. We study relatively simple organisms with relatively simple histories and under relatively simple environmental conditions. In this way we obtain the degree of rigour necessary for a scientific analysis. Our data are as uniform and reproducible as, say, the data of modern biology. It is true that the simplicity is to some extent artificial. We do not often find anything like it outside the laboratory — especially in the field of human behaviour, which is of primary interest. As a result those who are impatient to get on to bigger issues are inclined to object to the 'oversimplified' formulations of the laboratory.(*SHB*, pp. 204 – 5)

This approach has indeed been successful in the physical sciences, nor is Skinner the first to argue in favour of its application in psychology. It goes back to Hobbes and Descartes in the seventeenth century. Galileo 'homogenised' (his word) physics by disregarding surface differences between celestical and terrestrial motions. In the same way, Hobbes hoped psychology would be 'homogenised' by reducing all actions to bodily movements, explaining these movements with reference to the operation of underlying physical mechanisms. The behaviourist Hull advocated the same approach. A science of behaviour, he writes, must 'begin with colourless movements and mere receptor impulses as such' and proceeds to explain purposive human behaviour in terms of 'postulates involving mere stimuli and mere movement' (1943, pp. 25–26). The only thing that is new in Skinner is the mechanisms, namely operant reinforcement and extinction, which work on 'colourless movements' of which the neck-stretching of the pigeon is a paradigm.

Galileo was applying his paradigm of the ball rolling down an inclined plane to other cases of motion. There were various factors influencing the motion, the changes in velocity and direction, which were negligible or absent in the case of the fall down the inclined plane. This is the kind of simplicity which his paradigm cases possessed. The laws he formulated in his study of such simple cases were applicable to the complex cases in that the differences observed between them could be attributed to complicating factors not operating in the simple cases.

This is not, however, the kind of difference there is between the pigeon's behaviour in Skinner's experiment and human conduct. The difference here is not one of complexity. It is a *conceptual* difference. We identify, grasp, see and think of human conduct in terms of concepts which have no place in connection with the pigeon's behaviour. One cannot purge the language in which we talk about human conduct of these concepts, as Skinner proposes to do, and pretend that one is continuing to talk about *the same thing*. Human conduct and the pigeon's behaviour are not conceptually commensurable.

Skinner does not recognise this. He argues that there is nothing remarkable in developing a language of psychology that is different from the language of common sense. We find the same difference in physics. It is, of course, true that although sciences take their start from everyday language and the reality of certain questions asked in it, that language is often gradually modified beyond recognition by the introduction of new concepts and new systems of classification. But such modifications are *extensions* of the old language, and its new questions presuppose the reality of the questions asked in the common-sense language. Physicists continue to speak that language in their everyday lives. They do not reject it, as Eddington seemed to think. They cannot do so without undermining the intelligibility of the language of theoretical physics.

This is what Skinner does not understand. For his language of operant conditioning is not an extension of the everyday language in which we talk about ourselves and our conduct. What we have is not a conceptual extension, but a conceptual *break*. With that break we can no longer talk in the new language about the realities of human conduct which we refer to in the old one. Whereas the physicist who talks about the flow of electrons is still saying something relevant to the current which lights our bulbs and drives our engines.

3. Human and animal behaviour

In 'Behaviourism at Fifty', Skinner gives an argument for the rejection of consciousness which runs as follows: Man had always been thought of as essentially different from animals. Plato had thought of man as possessing a soul. Aristotle had thought of him as possessing the capacity for reasoning. Descartes had thought of him as capable of thought and intelligent action, and of brutes as automata. Darwin had established the continuity of the species and questioned this belief. If man is not essentially different from animals then either animals are like man, i.e. capable of thought, or man is like animals, i.e. his actions can be explained without reference to reason. Lloyd Morgan questioned the former alternative with his Canon of Parsimony: It is more economical to explain animal behaviour without resorting to the asumption of thought in them. Thorndike provided such an explanation. If evidence of consciousness can be explained in other ways in animals, why not also in man? Skinner considers himself to have done so by means of operant conditioning.

But this argument is spurious. One needs to ask: (1) What were Plato, Aristotle, and Descartes getting at? (2) What was it that Darwin established? (3) Are the two incompatible? Admittedly this is an oversimplification, since there are many differences between Plato, Aristotle and Descartes. But my point is this. Descartes may have been wrong to regard animals as automata. Aristotle may have been wrong in drawing a sharp line between man and animals in the way he did. But why should one not admit that there are many continuities between man and animals, that between the lower animals and man we have a whole spectrum of different overlaps, and still insist that there are important differences between man and even the higher animals, including apes?

Certainly it is not so much a question of choosing the most economical explanation, as it is of choosing the one that makes sense. Some of the explanations offered by pet owners in the anecdotes to which Skinner refers make no sense. That is the trouble with them. But this is equally the case with most of the explanations offered by Skinner of human behaviour. They are just as absurd. It is not that there is no such thing as operant conditioning, or that it does not apply to human behaviour, but that its scope there is very limited. Skinner is right to object to the simple-mindedness exhibited in the anecdotes of pet owners. We could label this simple-mindedness 'anthropomorphism'. But in his account of human behaviour Skinner exhibits the same kind of simple-mindedness in the opposite direction. We could label it 'animo-centricism'. There is nothing in Darwin to foster, let alone justify, such simple-mindedness.

Darwin collected his enormous catalogue of facts with love, patience, and an open mind. If Skinner had shown Darwin's application, care, patience and intelligence in his examination of human behaviour he could not possibly have tried to subsume it all under one blanket explanation. The truth is that Skinner does not approach his material in a truly empirical fashion, despite all show to the contrary. His reductionist zeal, his programmatic commitment, make that impossible.

He completely misunderstands what philosophers are up to when they 'attribute' consciousness, thought and intention to man. They are not advancing an explanatory hypothesis which can be subjected to scientific tests. They are concerned with articulating our conception of ourselves, to make explicit the 'grammar' of our talk about human conduct. Nothing that Darwin said touches that. What Darwin established was the evolutionary continuity between the species, between man and the lower animals, through the hierarchy of the animal kingdom. If one accepts this, one would expect to find different similarities between the hierarchy of species. But it would be foolish to expect the *same* similarities to run through all species. Darwin never made such a claim.

Certainly it does not follow from anything he said that we can explain the behaviour of members of the different species, men and all the different animals, in terms of the *same* concepts. Nor are psychologists justified in drawing the conclusion that animal experiments conducted in psychological laboratories can throw decisive light on human psychology. To think otherwise is like thinking that if, as Freud claimed, there is a developmental continuity between child and adult psychology then it follows that nothing new can come into adult life, that nothing can be found that was not there from the start.

People have attributed this thought to Freud; but I believe it to be a mistake. What confuses people is that Freud held, in addition, that the individual's emotional development is, more often than we recognise, arrested in various respects. When this is so, the adult's behaviour is governed by a childish mentality which he has not grown out of though he does not wish to own up to it. His behaviour can then be understood in terms of categories internal to this mentality. Hence the form of many psycho-analytic interpretations. There is, however, nothing comparable to this in the case of the evolutionary continuity between the species. For the continuity there holds between species, whereas Freud was talking about the relation between stages of the same individual's life — stages which can be remembered by him.

Just as the developmental continuity between the adult and the child does not exclude the possibility of much that is new coming into the adult's life, similarly the evolutionary continuity between the species does not exclude the possibility of much that is new characterising human life. The big difference comes with man's use of language and the way this use permeates all aspects of human life. It makes man's life the kind of life it is, and man the kind of creature he is. Almost all the capacities which Skinner denies to man in his reductionist analysis of psychological concepts, all the possibilities he rejects for man without even recognising them, are connected with the difference which the use of language makes to human life. Or rather I should say that everything that constitutes this difference is internal to human life. For what is in question is what we mean by 'human life'.

It is certainly very different from the sense in which talk of an animal's life, even that of a pet who has, as we say, become 'a member of the family'. Thus if I may formulate a question reminiscent of the one Wittgenstein asks in the *Philosophical Investigations* (p. 174):

One can say of a pet, a dog, that it is gentle, affectionate, faithful, not spoilt. One can attribute to him some of the good qualities we attribute to human beings. But can one admire or respect it? And why not? Again, one can easily imagine a dog missing the companion he had got attached to, or longing for his master's return and pining for him. But can we imagine him capable of the kind of love that is capable of suffering betrayal? (see Rhees, 1969, pp. 121–2)

Some psychologists have argued that apes are capable of acquiring a language (Linden, 1981). None of the observations or arguments in that book convinces me. But this is not the point. For us to imagine a colony of apes to be speaking a language there is a great deal we would have to imagine as different in their lives. The point is that if we did, then what we imagine would be very different from the picture which Skinner sketches of human and animal behaviour. There is no place in Skinner's conceptual framework for what we would have to imagine in order to imagine apes speaking a language.

But what about human language? Does Skinner allow that? And how could he not do so? The answer is that he may call what he allows 'language', but his account of both the learning and the use of language is as pathetic as his account of the rest of human behaviour. I have mentioned a few examples — his analysis of 'Come to dinner' and of 'That's right'. But I have not discussed his analysis of language as 'verbal behaviour', nor of how it is acquired by means of operant conditioning and of what speaking amounts to. I have said enough, however, to make it plain why I think he could not possibly do justice to what is involved in learning to speak, coming to have something to say, and carrying a conversation with someone.

To return to Darwin. I remarked that nothing that he said about the evolutionary continuity between species can touch our concept of ourselves as different from animals in those respects that are reflected in the 'grammar' of that aspect of our language which Skinner subjects to conceptual surgery. This is not to say that it cannot play a part in modifying our conception of ourselves in certain other respects. It may play a part in altering our attitude to nature and to animals. It may change our conception of our relations to nature. It may, indeed, have played a part in undermining certain religious and pseudo-religious beliefs, and in enhancing others. But this is a different matter and one from which Skinner is not justified in deriving any comfort.

What I am speaking of is a historical phenomenon, rather than a logical one — not a question of what further beliefs the acceptance of a theory or hypothesis commits one to. I am thinking of conceptual modification and erosion as a historical process. Skinner, himself, if enough people are taken in by him, may play a part in such a process of changing attitudes. It is more likely, however, that he is the *product* of such a process rather than the initiator of it, a process that flows at different levels. The movement on the surface, where Skinner's ideas enter into people's thinking, is a tidal one — back and forth. It is about twenty years since the tide has turned and behaviourism has been overtaken by cognitivism. But I venture to say that at a deeper level, the current is flowing in the same direction, that of a greater dehumanisation of academic psychology. For psychologists are, on one hand, no nearer to understanding the philosophical problems that run deep in psychology, and on the other they are too deeply submerged in the life of their times to be critical of the trends which they reflect in their work.

I am speaking of academic psychology. I have said nothing here about clinical psychology.

II
John Searle: a Materialistic Dualist

11
The Mind and the Body

1. Searle's problem and his simple solution

In his 1984 Reith Lectures on 'Minds, Brains and Science', Searle's 'overriding theme . . . concerns the relationship of human beings to the rest of the universe' (p. 8). This relationship poses for Searle the problem of reconciling the different conceptions we take of its two terms: our 'commonsense picture of ourselves as human beings' and our 'overall "scientific" conception of the physical world' (p. 13).

According to the latter — let me call it 'scientific materialism' — 'the world contains *nothing but* unconscious physical particles' (p. 13, my italics). But if so (Searle is puzzled) how can it '*also* contain consciousness'? (my italics). As he poses the question later: 'it is hard to see how mere physical systems could have consciousness' (p. 15). Again: 'How can a mechanical universe contain intentionalistic human beings — that is, human beings that can represent the world to themselves?' (p. 13). 'How can atoms in the void represent anything?' (p. 16)

These questions arise, not because Searle takes the physical sciences seriously, which he does and rightly so, but because he adheres to a certain metaphysical position. Without the desire to give 'a systematic description of the whole of reality' in terms of material particles the particular questions that puzzle Searle would not arise. Yet, if I am right, to do so is no part of the brief of the physical sciences.

For Searle, these questions narrow down to the question of the relation between the mind and the body, and even further, to that of the relation between the mind and the brain: How can the brain in my skull, a physiological organ, a purely material thing, be conscious? (p. 15) How can it be *about* anything, refer to anything? (p. 16) This is the question of how a mere physical system can have consciousness, represent anything. Because for Searle everything ultimately reduces to a physical system, the only possible subject for consciousness and intentionality becomes the brain. His metaphysics thus leads him to hold some very odd views.

Searle at no point sheds any of his metaphysical baggage, nor sees anything wrong in the way he formulates the questions he asks. He offers 'solutions' to his problems, not by retracing his steps and asking how he came to be where he stands, but by inventing new conceptual structures. These structures, expressed in the form of theses, 'solve' Searle's problems. At least *he* thinks so. But they are highly abstract and, at least prima facie, very implausible, to say the least.

Searle sees the problem of the relation between the mind and the body or brain as a scientific problem, the solution of which has been delayed for centuries by philosophical prejudice: 'How can we account for the relationship between two apparently completely different kinds of things?' (p. 14). He thinks of the removal of this prejudice as genuine philosophical work: 'the mind and the body . . . are not two different things' (p. 26). More than this, he thinks there are apparent conflicts between the theses he offers as his solution, and he regards the conceptual clarification which clears these up as also part of the philosophical task at hand (see p. 20). But he thinks of these general theses as part of the conceptual speculation that belongs to the sciences.

I glean all this from the various things he says. Thus he asks, 'Why do we still have in philosophy and psychology after all these centuries a "mind–body problem" in a way that we do not have, say, a "digestion–stomach problem"?' (p. 14). He clearly thinks that once this problem is solved, scientific enquiry can progress unhampered into such questions as 'What exactly is the neurophysiology of consciousness?' (p. 9). He clearly believes that once this clarification has been completed, it will become apparent that 'there are no logical or philosophical or metaphysical obstacles to account for the relation between the mind and the brain in terms that are quite familiar to us from the rest of nature' (p. 22). Providing such an account, then, is a task that belongs to the natural sciences.

Searle further believes that, as a result, what appears mysterious will cease to appear so: 'Why does the mind [or consciousness]

seem more mysterious than other biological phenomena?' (p. 14).
'The way . . . to dispel the mystery is to understand the processes'
(p. 23) — in this case, how 'processes [in the brain] cause consciousness' (p. 24). This question, as he sees it, belongs to the
'neurophysiology of consciousness'.

Seeing the 'mind–body problem' in this way Searle offers what
he regards as 'a rather simple solution, one that is consistent both
with what we know about neurophysiology and with our common-
sense conception of the nature of mental states — pains, beliefs,
desires and so on' (p. 14). He regards this solution to be consonant
with his scientific materialism, a position he never questions. He
also believes that, unlike other forms of materialistic conceptions of
the mind, his solution does not 'downgrade the status of mental
entities' (p. 15). For it gives explicit recognition to those 'four
features of mental phenomena which have made them seem
impossible to fit into our ''scientific'' conception of the world as
made up of material things' (p. 15), namely 'consciousness',
'intentionality', 'subjectivity' (or 'the asymmetrical logic of the
mind' as I prefer to call it after John Wisdom), and 'mental
causation' (that feature which is denied by epi-phenomenalism).

Searle's solution works, he believes, because it meets the very
requirements which created his problem in the first place: it is
materialistic and yet it preserves the unique status of the mind. It
allows for a two-way causal interaction between the mind and the
body without regarding these as 'two different things' (p. 26). It
does so by identifying the mind and the brain at the micro-level,
while regarding the mind, consisting of unique properties at the
macro-level, as resulting from micro-processes in the brain.

Thus his two theses: (1) 'All mental phenomena are *caused* by
processes in the brain' (p. 18). (2) All mental phenomena are 'just
features of the brain' (p. 19). He elucidates, in terms of examples,
the scientific model which suggests these two theses, examines the
concept of causality involved in the first thesis, and in this way
argues for their compatibility. He then goes on to discuss, briefly,
the difficulties which his 'four features of the mind' pose for the
possibility of any relation between the mind and the body: (1) How
is consciousness possible in a material world? (2) How can atoms
in the void have intentionality? (3) How can there be any place for
subjectivity in an objective world? (4) How can mental events
cause physical events? He answers these questions within the
framework of his general solution.

I will select three of Searle's claims for critical discussion, namely his two theses and his idea of 'mental causation'. These are the most distinctive features of his account. I find what he says on these completely unconvincing; indeed these three claims strike me as complete 'philosophical fiction'. I shall try to make plain why I think so. I shall finish by indicating how I see the so-called mind–body problem and of what sort of 'solution' it is susceptible.

2. Can 'mental phenomena' be caused by brain processes?

I use inverted commas round the 'philosophical' expression 'mental phenomena'. I know that Searle uses it as a short-hand expression for pains, beliefs, desires and thoughts, and he would add 'and the like' or 'and so on'. This is so common in philosophy that we think we understand 'and the like' when we do not. Indeed, what Searle mentions here is a mixed bag. The idea of 'mental phenomena' conjures up the idea of sparks flying inside one's head, but in a special medium, 'visible' to none but the person in question. Sparks flying are phenomena, and what makes them special makes them 'mental'. This is part of the Cartesian picture which needs criticism and rejection.

Thinking, for instance, of physical pain in this way, as one kind of mental phenomenon, it becomes plausible to think of it as the end-product of certain physico-chemical changes in the nervous system. This way of thinking is crucial to Searle's first thesis, as we shall see. But what is wrong with it?

Someone may protest: Is not a sensation, say pain, the effect of a physical stimulus, as when a person touches a flame? The physico-chemical processes in the body, produced by the burning, in turn cause the pain. And this, surely, is a mental occurrence, if anything is.

Here we have the idea of pain as a self-contained occurrence, in a private world to which only the person in pain has access, an occurrence cut off from the public world in which we live. So conceived, we think of pain as the terminus of a chain of causes. We know how the impulse travels along the nerve, what part of the brain it reaches, and what goes on in the brain as a result. What we do not know (we think) is how the brain processes, thus produced, give rise to the private occurrence we name 'pain'. This is the problem tackled by Searle.

Of course it is perfectly appropriate to talk of the *cause* of pain, to say that the touching of the flame *caused* the person in question some pain. But what does this mean? How do we normally understand it? And what does it mean to say of this person that he feels pain? It means, surely, that he reacts in the way he does — he pulls his hand away immediately, with a shout or groan, his face twists in agony, he holds his hand out, blows on it or dips it in cold water. All this is part of what we *mean*. To say that his pain was caused by the flame means that the flame burned his hand ('to burn' being a causal verb) and that what I have just described is his reaction to being burnt. That reaction, I repeat, is a reaction of pain.

I said of what I described that it is part of what we *mean* by 'being in pain'. What Descartes did (and Searle follows in his footsteps) is to isolate what we mean by 'being in pain' from all this and to think of what I have described as merely the bodily symptoms of pain — much in the way that high temperature and nausea may be symptoms of an inflamed appendix. The appendix can be removed, examined and its inflammation seen apart from the bodily symptoms the patient describes to the doctor. Similarly, we are inclined to think that those who see the symptoms of pain cannot be in contact with the pain itself, in the way the surgeon is with the inflamed appendix when it lies open to view. For the appendix is a public, physical object, whereas the pain is a private, mental occurrence. Only the person himself cognises it in what he feels. It is *that* which is the pain, and the bodily symptoms which give others an indication of it are *external* to the pain.

There is something right about this, and also something badly wrong, and the two are entangled. Of course the pain in question is something only the person in pain *feels*, and the reactions I have mentioned are not 'what he feels'. Besides, he could feel the pain and not exhibit these reactions. They are 'expressions' of the pain he feels. But that does not make them 'external' to the pain.

This idea is part of the source of our problems. For it leads us to think that each person learns what pain is *from his own case*. He identifies an inner occurrence and names it 'pain', and each time he recognises the occurrence in question he is justified in calling it 'pain' — 'justified before himself' as Wittgenstein puts it. In *Philosophical Investigations*, he has shown conclusively that this claim involves insuperable difficulties and on examination turns out to be incoherent. I will not now repeat his argument.

I said that I can keep the pain I feel to myself, check my natural inclination to groan or wince. This does not make what I *mean* by the word 'pain' something I cannot convey to other people. Nor does it mean that how people react when in pain and how they respond to someone else's reactions of pain play no role in my learning this meaning. It is tautologically true that the pain I feel is *my* pain and that it is something I *can* suffer silently, provided it is not too great; but the *meaning* of the word I use when I want someone else to know is *public*. It is a word in a public language, one which I have learned like anyone else. The language, the meaning exists independently of me, and I do not learn it *from my own case*. My exposition to other people's reactions in certain situations as well as to their reactions to mine is crucial to my learning to use the word and understand its meaning. If I were cut off from all this, however often I may feel pain I would not learn to *tell* others, nor consequently to think that I am in pain when I am, to hold it before my mind.

Having shown the incoherence of the idea of a 'private identification' Wittgenstein goes on to suggest how in the first place we come to learn the meaning of the word 'pain'. A child falls down, hurts himself, and comes running to his parents crying, perhaps holding the part of the body that hurts. Wittgenstein calls this 'the natural, primitive behaviour or expression of pain'. It is not something the child learns. His parents respond by attending to the part of his body that hurts, comforting him, and he hears them use the word 'pain' or 'hurts'. The next time the child falls down and comes running to his parents he uses the word he has heard them use in this connection. Wittgenstein says that what the child learns is not to identify something, but to give verbal expression to his pain. The verbal expression replaces the natural, primitive expression, and it serves the same role. His parents respond to it in the same way that they responded to his behavioural expression in the first place. The sentence 'I am in pain' or 'It hurts,' as it is first learned, thus does not describe anything; it gives expression to the pain which the speaker feels, much like 'Ouch!', a groan, or any other exclamation.

The *meaning* of the word 'pain', like any other word, is to be found in the way it is used in such sentences, and the sentences are learned and used in public circumstances, in the weave of pain behaviour and other people's responses to such behaviour. There is nothing private, therefore, about the meaning of the word 'pain'. Secondly, there is nothing private about the pain in which the child comes running to his parents. The parents are in no doubt about the child's pain, and they do not feel cut off from it, in the way one feels cut off from someone who retires into himself or cannot give expression to what he feels. They do not think, 'These are only outward signs of pain', like the smoke from a fire they cannot see. Their child's pain is perfectly transparent to them.

Pain, when it is not hidden from other people, is visible to them. It is and can be *seen* from outside. The person in pain *feels* it. Pain is thus something felt by the person in pain and seen by others when this person does not keep it to himself. Descartes wrongly thought of pain as something that can only be felt. He forgot that it can also be seen by others.

What I called 'expressions of pain' (facial, postural, vocal, behavioural) are that *in* which pain becomes visible to others. These expressions (Hampshire, 1961) are originally *constitutive* of pain. For the young child who comes running to his mother crying, these natural reactions are an inseparable part of the whole situation in which he learns to use the word 'pain'. The word thus relates to them in the way I suggested, so that what we call 'feeling pain' or 'being in pain' and these reactions belong together and form a single unity. To the child the pain he feels is not yet something he can consider or keep to himself. The sentence he learns to utter is not used as a description for the benefit of others from whom what is described is hidden.

It is only as he learns to speak and to utter such sentences as exclamations alongside or in place of the natural, primitive reactions of pain that these reactions become *voluntary* in certain circumstances. It is only as he learns to express his feelings verbally that he becomes capable of hiding them. Hiding one's feelings thus is not something negative, like omitting to report what others cannot see. It is a positive action — one suppresses one's natural reactions and checks the expression of pain. Hidden pain then is what *remains* of what originally belonged together, and still does in our *concept* of pain, constituting what we understand by 'being in pain'.

The Cartesian conception of pain, therefore, as a state divorced from and only accidentally connected with pain behaviour, identifiable in separation from anything physical, is defective. Yet it is pain *so conceived* that is thought to be caused by physico-chemical phenomena in the body. We are then puzzled as to how physico-chemical processes in the body can give rise to pain, an item of consciousness, and how that in turn can cause a bodily movement. This is how the mind–body problem presents itself to Searle.

But this is to misconstrue what we mean when we say, 'His pain was caused by the flame he touched.' What is in question is *not* one of the links (albeit maverick, because it is mental) in a chain of events causally linked. No; what is in question is a person coming to be in pain, and this, namely his being in pain, is *not* 'the occurrence of some private state of consciousness', 'a mental phenomenon'. It is what he feels and what others see in his reactions. It is not *because* he is in pain that he reacts this way, but rather his reacting this way in the circumstances is part of what we mean by his being in pain. The reaction is his response to his hand being burnt. The pain is *in* his reaction, and this is the reaction of a person or animal. It is not some process or event alongside the physico-chemical changes in the body. Those could conceivably take place in organic matter and their identification does not presuppose the life of a person or animal. Whereas in separation from the reactions of a person or animal one cannot speak of pain, no matter what physico-chemical changes take place in the 'organism'.

So what burning *causes* in this case is not something one can describe without referring to the man or animal. It is *he* who feels the pain, who shouts and writhes. This is the kind of *effect* we have here, *not* the kind of event that forms a link in a chain that includes the secretion of acetylcholine by nerve cells at synapses.

Of course those physico-chemical changes take place, and if they did not, the man who touches the flame would feel no pain — just as when the retina is detached from the optic nerve a man does not see, or when he is paralysed he cannot move his limbs at will. Seeing, willing, and having pain can only be intelligibly attributed to human beings and to other creatures who behave like human beings. They are not occurrences or states, identifiable in isolation from the kind of behaviour and circumstances with which we are familiar in human and, to some extent, in animal life. They are not the kind of thing that can be said to be produced by physico-chemical processes in the organism. No, the pain the man feels has been caused by burning his hand upon touching a flame, and the physico-chemical processes are necessary for the flame to cause him pain in the sense that what interferes with these processes stops the pain — like an anaesthetic.

One could say that the body and the mind are intimately involved in pain and in other sensations, but very differently from the way pictured by the dualist. The body comes in for the person who feels pain in that he feels the pain in this or that part of his body. That is why we speak of the sensation of pain as 'physical pain'. Yet it characterises or is related to the painful spot differently from the way a visible property, such as a colour, characterises or is related to the visible spot. This is part of what makes philosophers say that pain is a *mental* phenomenon whereas the colour of the visible spot is a *physical* property.

Thus when I hold my cheek and shout when the dentist pokes the cavity in my tooth *I* am the one who feels the pain, and the reactions in which this finds expression are *mine*; the groan comes out of my mouth, the tears stream down my cheeks. If the tears are to be fought, the groan to be checked, the person who does so is me. And if the pain becomes unbearable I am the person to whom the dentist gives an anaesthetic. We thus use the personal pronoun in speaking of it — I speak of it as 'my pain' and you refer to it as 'his' or use my name.

In contrast, when I look at and gesture towards the sunset and marvel at the colour of the sky, what I am gesturing towards is something that you can see too. What you say you see and what I say I see are one and the same thing; its identity involves no reference to you or me or anybody else. It is the colour of the sky.

The body of the person in pain comes into our conception of pain then through the way it provides a place for the pain, and through the bodily expressions that fall under the domain of his will, so that he can to some extent hide his pain from others. It also comes in through the physiological processes without which no injury to the body would cause him to feel pain. Finally, in the case of another person's pain, the body comes into my conception of it in that it is in his features, expressions, postures, tone of voice and other reactions that I see his pain.

I have argued against Searle's way of conceiving pain as a mental occurrence or phenomenon. This is the Cartesian conception, not the way we think of it in our day-to-day life. Yet it is only when so conceived that we try to relate it to physiological processes as cause and effect in a way that is truly puzzling. It is this puzzle which Searle attempts to solve without rejecting, or at least examining, the conceptual structure which supports it, a structure which is the product of certain deep-seated philosophical presuppositions.

His 'simple argument' for the claim that 'all of our thoughts and feelings are caused by processes inside the brain' rests on this structure: 'If the events outside the central nervous system occurred, but nothing happened in the brain, there would be no mental events. But if the right things happened in the brain, the mental events would occur even if there was no outside stimulus'

(p. 19). Yes, it is true that you could produce certain pains and sensations in a person or animal by the electrical stimulation of his brain, and even perhaps certain visions and thoughts in the case of a person capable of perception and thought. All right, the 'peripheral' nervous impulses are not necessary. But this does not mean that the rest of the body, that of a person or animal, the face, the mouth, the eyes in which sensations normally find expression are superfluous, not necessary. Nor, in the case of perceptions, however hallucinatory, and thoughts, does it mean that all that the person has learnt to be capable of seeing things and thinking about them can be dispensed with as 'peripheral' or 'accidental'. The argument completely ignores everything that is logically presupposed in attributing pain, perception and thought to a person, including pain in a phantom limb.

The case of pain is, of course, superficially the most plausible example for Searle's first thesis, since we talk of the cause of pain, and what causes it is also what causes the nervous impulses which reach the brain. There is not even any prima facie plausibility for the idea of thinking, seeing or hearing as the end product of a causal series. I have argued the case for perception elsewhere and I will not repeat now what I said there.[1] As for thinking — a voluntary activity 'intentionally' directed to the 'object' of one's thoughts — how can that be the causal product of a physiological process?

It is true that my thoughts can be affected by drugs. I may become confused in my thoughts, or thoughts that are confused may become clear. What the drug does is to affect, favourably or adversely, the causal, physiological background necessary for a person to think at all. But these physiological conditions causally necessary to thinking are *not* the cause of a person's thoughts, in the way that a derangement in the inner ear may be the cause of the ringing in a person's ear. It doesn't make sense to speak of the cause of a thought; a thought in my head is not like a ringing in my ear. You can cause me to think or, more naturally, you can give me a cause for thought. Here it is I, as a person, that you challenge or provoke, and my thinking, my attempt to come to terms with the question you have raised in your challenge is my response to it. This is very different indeed from giving me a drug. As I said, the drug does not cause me to think, in the way that your question does — I don't know what that would mean — it affects my thinking. And when it does, *I* am still the one who does the thinking. Until I have learned to do so, no drug can get me to think.

Let me return to the case of pain, a pain in my hand, caused by the electrical stimulation of the brain. Here what is in question is not a stimulus in the sense in which the flame that burns my hand is — if, indeed, it is a 'stimulus' at all properly speaking. At any rate, far from being a more direct or 'proximate' stimulus, as Searle thinks, it is experientially an indirect stimulus only. It certainly does not cause the pain in the same sense that the flame does. For pain is a localised sensation and what we regard as its cause, its direct cause so to speak, works on that locality — a blow, a cut, a burning of the flesh.

We have seen that Searle thinks of pain as the 'mental' effect of a physical cause. He then wishes to reconcile this kind of dualism with scientific materialism. He parts company with Descartes at this point. He says that the chain of causes comes to an end with the electrical processes in the brain at the micro-level — the firing of the neurons there. There is no *further* event at *this* level. Pain is simply the manifestation of this *same* event at the macro-level. This is Searle's second thesis. Pain, and all other 'mental phenomena', are properties of the brain at the macro-level, properties which have just those features which make them 'mental properties'. But this, as I will try to show, is a metaphysical sleight of hand.

The difference between Searle and Descartes could be expressed diagrammatically as follows:

Descartes: physical stimulus → nerve impulses → brain processes cause$_1$
→   pain as a 'mental phenomenon'

pain as a 'mental phenomenon'

↑   cause$_2$

Searle: physical stimulus → nerve impulses → brain processes

It is in the way they think of the relation between brain processes and pain that Searle and Descartes differ from each other. For Descartes, the causal relation is a 'same-level', event-to-event, Humean causation. For Searle, it is what he calls a 'bottom-up' type of causation which he explains in terms of examples from physics — e.g. the liquid state of water at room temperature as the causal outcome of its molecular structure.

But there is no genuine analogy here between the two cases. The comparison is wholly artificial, and Searle resorts to it as a means of solving his problem. The last link in the Cartesian chain has been found difficult to stomach, and Searle's 'ingenious' solution is to deflect the flow of causes when the last link is reached and, simultaneously, to change the character of this link.

The analysis I have suggested is not dualistic and rejects Cartesian dualism. It can be represented schematically as follows:

Flame touching a person's hand → The person feeling pain in his hand

Normal physiological
conditions necessary for
the person to feel pain
when his hand touches a
flame

The direct causal link is not between 'events in different media' or 'at two different levels'. The idea that it is so is a philosophical fiction which is the product of certain presuppositions. This perfectly ordinary link is discovered by us experientially as children. The physiological conditions are discovered and studied by scientists. They discover, for instance, that the injection of certain substances into the bloodstream can disturb the normal processes in operation when, for instance, a person feels a burning pain in his hand. They investigate how and where these processes are affected by such substances and build up a picture of the many different points at which they can be so disturbed. In this way they come to know how each disturbance can be caused and how such disturbances can be remedied.

This is how I see the relation between the expert's knowledge of human physiology and our everyday, experiential, unproblematic knowledge of ourselves.

Before going on to criticise Searle's even less plausible second thesis, let me make some comments on the sense in which we talk of the causes of our emotions, for the sense in which an insult, for instance, may make someone angry, or hurtful words may cause one pain is very different from the sense in which cuts and blows hurt people.

3. Emotions, their causes and the body

How are we to think of the relation between an emotion and what arouses it? How are we to think of the relation between an emotion and the bodily, physiological expressions of that emotion?

If we categorise an emotion as 'something mental' it is then very easy to think of it as a 'mental state' — the way in which we think of pain as a 'mental occurrence'. We then think of its causation in something like the following way. We have a series of phenomena, some physical and some mental, with causal links between them, for instance:

(i) Someone insults me. This is thought of as an 'external' phenomenon, something environmental that impinges on my sense organs in the form of physical stimuli.

(ii) This causes me to feel angry. Thus a physical phenomenon gives rise to a mental state through the intermediary of my body.

(iii) In Hume this then gives my will an object so that I acquire an inclination or desire to strike the person who insulted me.

(iv) This, in turn, causes me to strike him — a movement of the arm.

Many psychologists and philosophers (introspectionists, behaviourists, and materialists) swallow this whole way of looking at human emotions and actions. The assumptions implicit in their thinking shape their conception of how human behaviour is to be studied. B. F. Skinner, for instance, says that since what we have here is a *causal series* of which the intermediate links are not subject to public scrutiny,

insult ⇸ anger → will to hit ⇸ hitting

we can ignore the middle terms without any loss to our investigation of the causes of emotional behaviour. William James moves within the same pattern of thought. For him, an emotion is a mental state akin to a sensation.

Once one views emotions in this way it is natural to think of the sequence in terms of causal links: insult → anger → striking and other bodily expressions — e.g. accelerated heartbeat. William James attributes this view to common sense and reverses the sequence:

Common sense says . . . we are insulted by a rival, are angry and strike. The hypothesis to be defended says that this order of sequence is incorrect, that the one mental state is not immediately induced by the other, that the bodily manifestations must first be interposed between, and that the more rational statement is that we feel angry because we strike, and not that we strike because we are angry. Without the bodily states following on the perception, the latter would be purely cognitive in form, pale, colourless, destitute of emotional warmth. We might then receive the insult and deem it right to strike, but we should not feel angry. (1948, pp. 375–6)

The two questions I wanted to comment on are here jumbled together because of James's failure to distinguish between the behaviour or affective response and the bodily expression of an emotion. This is no accident; it is part of James's reductionism:

(i) The reduction of emotional experience to sensations.
(ii) The reduction of emotional behaviour to reflex movements.

Having done so (in ii), no difference remains between the hitting seen as a reflex movement of the arm and the responses of the smooth muscles and glands — secretion of adrenalin, accelerated heartbeat, etc. Given these two reductions, James can only connect emotions and emotional responses so conceived as cause and effect — we are angry because we strike the person who insulted us. This is the only way in which the insult, thought of as a physical stimulus outside us, can be seen to affect our mental state, namely through the changes it produces in our bodies.

But James is wrong about what he calls the common-sense view — that is, if by this we are to understand our everyday conception of the matter, as this is embodied in the way we speak of it. True, the sequence is as he depicts it in the view he attributes to common sense. However, the common-sense view is *not* that anger is a state of mind, logically akin to sensation, one which has certain causal effects on us. This is only a particular *philosophical account* of it — and a defective one at that. The truth of the matter is that our anger is a response to the insult, which takes the form of wanting to retaliate in kind. Striking is the execution of this desire, except that normally there is no gap between the desire and the striking. The desire does not precede the striking and does not have a separate existence from it. It does so only when we refrain from giving way to it. We say that the striking is an *expression* of our anger. As such, it is part of what we understand by 'being angry', though it is not necessary to a person's being angry.

It is true that the connection between the insult and the angry response is a causal one: 'What he said made me angry.' But this is not like pulling the trigger of a gun and causing an explosion. This mechanical analogy which James uses (1948, p. 416) is only a metaphor. For the insult is *not* a 'physical phenomenon', it cannot be reduced to a pattern of sounds. It is (if I may put it so) a social phenomenon, and the person insulted grasps its sense, though doing so is not some 'inner happening'. The insult affects him through this sense which he grasps, given who he is, where he stands, and what he cares for. The insult and the angry response are part of a social interchange; the space or dimension in which the insult causes the insulted person to react angrily is a social dimension within which two people come in contact with each other as individuals. It is not a physical space within which mechanical causes operate.

There is this truth nevertheless in James's claim that I feel angry because I strike, feel frightened because I run away, namely that in striking the person who insults me, in running from the beast which frightens me, I give in to the emotion and thus affirm the reality which the insult or the danger has for me. Thus when I strike the person who insulted me, he becomes a monster in my imagination. This intensifies my anger and I want to strike him again. In contrast, in controlling my anger, though not in bottling it up, I keep a certain sense of proportion.

The insult, then, was indeed the cause of my anger. But if we now say that this is an instance of causal interaction between the body on which a physical stimulus impinges and the mind which is thrown into a state of anger we will have misconstrued (1) what it means to be insulted, (2) what it means to be angry, and (3) what it means to talk of the former as the cause of the latter. The anger, as I said, is *in* my response; that response is an expression of the anger I feel. In the particular circumstances, my hitting him may be all that there is to my anger. Perhaps it may also include the look in my eyes and the thoughts in my head. The idea that there is some *one* thing, a special mental state, which *is* the anger is a common philosophical myth, and the question of how each one of us identifies it and whether our identifications coincide so that we can understand the meaning of the word each of us uses to name it flows from this myth.

As for what we mean by 'cause' here, we have seen that it is very different from a mechanical cause. The insult does not cause something in me, cause a mental state to come into being, a mental bulb to 'light up', as it were, when you press the right stop. The insult does not trigger off a reaction in some part of me, my mind, as a drug may trigger off a reaction in my stomach, for example, causing stomach cramps. It affects me as a person on account of its particular significance; it is I who respond to it in anger when I hit the person who insults me, and when I get upset in the way I do. It is part of this upset that the whole rhythm of my body is altered. The anger which is in my response, in my desire to retaliate, is a mode of consciousness or apprehension in that it is my grasp of the significance of the other man's words and action as an insult. It is the form which my apprehension of the significance of these as an insult directed to me takes, given that I am not indifferent. This is what we mean when we say, 'His words roused my anger.' The idea of his words as a stimulus which give rise to a mental state in me which is my anger is not even a caricature of what is in question.

I now turn to the so-called bodily symptoms of anger — the way I am gripped by anger physically, upset in my body, with my heart beating fast, the blood rushing to my face, my eyes feeling as if they are ready to pop out of their sockets. Both James and Skinner say that the emotion is simply the bodily feelings and sensations produced by these physiological phenomena.

These bodily phenomena and feelings exist of course, but they are not in themselves the anger that I feel, no more than this is so in the case of my hitting someone or my thinking that he has insulted me. They too are expressions of my anger — that is, of my grasp of the insult, of my recognition of it as directed to me, of my burning desire to retaliate. They are the way in which I am overwhelmed by this desire, the way in which my recognition comes home to me given my disposition — my pride or honour, the chip on my shoulder, my readiness to take offence. James is quite right when he says that where I am not upset bodily, that is, responding with my whole body, my grasp of the insult remains purely cognitive, mental or intellectual. But when I am touched, when the rhythm of my body is altered, I do not merely see the situation in which I am placed by being insulted; I grasp its reality 'in my guts', 'viscerally'. Indeed, I would say that my bodily reaction confers reality to the insult in my apprehension of it. Here we have one aspect of the relation between the somatic and the mental in connection with emotions. But my representation of it, which claims to be faithful to the logic of our everyday apprehension of these matters, involves no Cartesian dualism.

4. Can 'mental phenomena' be properties of the brain?

I now return to Searle. We have seen that he regards pains and and thoughts, emotions and perceptions, without distinction, conceived of as 'mental phenomena', as the end product of chains of physiological events, causally linked, and concentrates on the last link. It is here that he differs from Descartes. He represents it as a bottom-up causal link on the model of the link between the molecular structure of a substance such as water and its physical properties accessible to our senses. These latter are 'caused' by the molecular structure of water, by the mechanical properties of the molecules, and yet they are properties of water — its wetness and liquidity for instance. These properties belong to the water at the macro-level; they do not characterise the molecules themselves. Whatever description we may give at the micro-level, this description would not, and indeed could not, intelligibly include any reference to such properties. Similarly, Searle argues, the 'mental phenomena' caused by brain processes — a way of talking I have criticised — are properties of the brain', sensible presumably to 'introspection',[2] inescapably so, and as such with those distinctive features, the denial of which would constitute the downgrading of the mind.

As I said before, I see no similarity at all between what Searle compares here. The only analogy I can construct leads me in a very different direction. No doubt the brain of a person has a micro-structure of its own, and the stimulation of his sensory receptors, or the direct electrical stimulation of his brain, would bring about certain changes in this micro-structure. If these changes are detectable at all by the senses at the macro-level, in analogy with Searle's examples from physics, they will have to be properties detectable symmetrically by any observer. The person whose brain is in question will have to detect it by some arrangement which will enable him to see his own brain in a mirror or on the screen of some sophisticated instrument.

But why not say that the sensation of pain, for instance, which may indeed be caused in this way, is the person's awareness of what is taking place in his brain? For the simple reason that the sensation is not a sensation in the brain. At best the sensation thus produced is a signal that something is going on in his brain.

Descartes spoke of our sensations as 'confused perceptions' of parts of our body, as in the case where I know that my hand is being burnt or cut without looking at it and without seeing the flame or the knife. What is involved here is a mixture of pain in a particular locality of my body, a pain with a particular content, and a genuine perception by touch of the object causing the pain. My brain, however, is not sensitive to touch in this way, it is not an organ of perception. Nor, as I said, is the pain produced by its electrical stimulation felt as a pain inside my head, in my brain.

In any case, where my hand is being cut or burnt, the pain I feel there is not a property of my hand. It is not a *property* at all, as the cut there, the burn, the bruise or other injury on the spot that hurts is. I may at the time be 'a man in pain'. But it would be ludicrous to construe the pain I feel either as a property I have as a person, however transitory, or as itself the property of something I perceive, which is the damage to my hand.

I may not, of course, show the pain I feel or give expression to it. All the same, the *possibility* of my having pains at all, pains which I can keep to myself, as well as that of your attributing such pains to me, is bound up with my *reacting* to painful stimuli. The sense of 'pain' that we understand by the word, we have already seen, cannot be severed from such responses. How can you attribute pain to a creature who never ducks blows, never winces or cries when it burns or cuts itself, receives blows or kicks? I do not see how pains could be 'realised' (as Searle puts it) in a brain, nor what 'realised' could mean here. Searle's examples from physics leave me no wiser in this respect.

As for a thought, how on earth can it be the property of a brain? A thought in any case is not a property at all. It is not a property of anything, not even of me as a person. I think my thoughts, much in the way that I do the various things which constitute the actions of which I am the agent. And I may think the same thought in different ways, in words in my head or in diagrams on a piece of paper. Indeed my thoughts are bound up with my actions in a way which needs elucidation. Certainly my relation to my thoughts is very different from the relation of a thing to its properties.

Furthermore, imagine my brain *in vitro* with exactly the same process going on in it as go on in my brain when I think. It would be ludicrous to suggest that some thinking is going on there. Not in the absence of the kind of life in which creatures like us carry on certain activities, exhibit reactions in the way we do to things which interest or affect it in various ways. *Who* is supposed to be doing the thinking here? What else is it supposed to be capable of doing which involves or requires thinking? In the brain you do not have the right kind of 'object' — an agent with a life and interests of its own — to which you can attribute thoughts, however well it 'ticks over'. This ticking over has little relevance to thinking in comparison with human actions and behaviour.

In short, what is caused by brain processes and realised in the system of neurons which constitute the brain, on the model of Searle's examples from physics, *cannot* be thoughts or sensations. Any serious reflection on what a thought or sensation is would establish that incontrovertibly.

Searle's two theses are sheer philosophical fantasy, a product of clever conceptual juggling. They bear no relation to the realities they are supposed to portray or provide an account of. They are the product of Searle's inventiveness, given his metaphysical needs. Even if we forget their incoherence and consider them as abstract conceptual theses or accounts, such as we find in the sciences, what good, what use are they to anyone? Do the scientist, the physiologist, the psychologist really need them? Certainly they may need to have their conceptual puzzles and perplexities resolved; that is different. But can they actually do anything with these theses? I very much doubt it. Searle's criticism of alternative accounts of the relation between the mind and the brain — 'strong AI' and 'weak AI' or 'cognitivism' — and his positive accounts of human action and the social sciences, in lectures 2 to 5, stand or fall independently of these theses, his 'solution' to the mind–body problem.

5. Mental causation

So far I have tried to show that Searle's claims for the one direction of the interaction between the mind and the body are confused. I now turn to his account of the other direction in which such causal interaction is supposed to take place, namely what he calls 'mental causation'.

Certainly Searle is right in wishing to resist any account of the mind in which its special status is downgraded, especially when it takes the form of epiphenomenalism. But this doesn't mean that there is such a thing as 'mental causation'. This is a Cartesian notion which belongs with Searle's notion of 'mental phenomena', 'mental events', and so on. What Searle is trying to capture by means of the notion of mental causation is the idea of human agency, the way it involves thoughts, the relation between intentions or decisions and human action.

Strangely, in view of much of what he says about intentions and actions in his fourth lecture, Searle presents the relation between an intention and an action in the first lecture in terms of a disembodied mental event, conceived as a cause, and a bodily movement, its effect, conceived as a physical motion. 'We all suppose', he writes, 'as part of common sense, that our thoughts and feelings make a real difference to the way we behave, that they actually have some *causal* effect on the physical world' (p. 17). It is worth pausing for a minute on what Searle is trying to say and on how he says it. What would it be like for our thoughts and feelings *not* to make a real difference to the way we behave? The kind of example that naturally springs to mind is the alcoholic who knows he is ruining his life and causing a lot of misery to his wife and children, for whose plight he has a lot of feeling, but who goes on getting drunk night after night *just the same*. This is clearly *not* the contrast which Searle has in mind. For the alcoholic's behaviour, though it contrasts with 'normal' behaviour, belongs to the same class, namely human behaviour. What it contrasts with is the 'behaviour' of inanimate things, such as physical motion studied by the physicist. It is this contrast which interests Searle, and in his attempt to understand what it comes to, he is led to represent human behaviour in terms of the Cartesian categories of mind and matter, conceived in separation from each other.

'Thoughts and feelings . . . have some *causal* effect on the physical world.' If we look at these words without mercy they will make no sense at all. Thoughts and feelings do not and cannot have any *causal* effect on the physical world. However much an architect may think about the house of his dreams, no house will sprout from the ground as a result. This has to be executed, put into practice by him, if the house is to materialise. The causal transaction takes place between the architect's *actions* and the builders and what goes on around them. They bring about things as a result of what they *do*. The causes in question are not thoughts and feelings, but actions into which these enter; and the actions are such things as carrying stones, mixing cement, and so on. The causal transactions in question are physical transactions initiated by men. Men are causal agents by virtue of their capacity to act, and they can only act as the flesh-and-blood creatures they are.

If those actions have causal effects which the men in question intend and plan, this doesn't mean that the actions themselves are the effects of something mental within the men, namely their thoughts and intentions. That is the Cartesian view which Searle swallows, not the so-called commonsense view. On the Cartesian view the connection between a disembodied intention, thought of as a mental state, and an action or voluntary movement, thought of as a physical motion or event, is a *magical* connection. It does not have the sense even of a causal connection: 'I decide to raise my arm and — lo and behold — my arm goes up (p. 17). It is no wonder that Searle is puzzled: 'if our thoughts and feelings are truly mental, how can they affect anything physical?' (ibid.).

The act, in the case of a voluntary movement, does not 'follow' my decision or intention, as if it were an event which I bring about by pressing the right mental button. My intentions and decisions are not the causes of what I do, conceived of as events I bring about. After all, I can form an intention and forever defer its execution. If, rather clumsily, I say that it is as a result of an intention that I did what I did, this simply is a way of denying the suggestion that I did it unintentionally — I intended those hurtful words, they were not a slip of the tongue; I meant to hurt him. This is not a matter of causality.

Thinking of it as such, however, Searle asks 'how mental events can cause physical events': 'how could anything as "weightless" and "ethereal" as a thought [presumably an intention] give rise to an action?' His answer is that 'thoughts are not weightless and ethereal. When you have a thought, brain activity is actually going on' (p. 25). He then uses his special identity thesis to explain how two different types of causality — ordinary physical causality and 'intentional' causality — operate at two different levels:

> Consciousness, for example, is a real property of the brain that can cause things to happen. My conscious attempt to perform an action such as raising my arm causes the movement of the arm. At the higher level of description, the intention to raise my arm causes the movement of the arm. But at the lower level of description, a series of neuron firings starts a chain of events that results in the contraction of the muscles. (p. 26)

As I have already suggested, what is claimed at the lower-level description may well be true. But what is being claimed here is related to what is claimed by the higher-level description in a very different manner from what Searle says. The firing of the neurons is a causally necessary condition for a person's moving his arm at will. Thus if, as in Hume's example, his arm has, unknown to him, suffered a paralysis he will fail to move it at will, to his consternation. As for the higher-level description, construed as giving a causal account, it is entirely bogus. It is so construed for no other reason than to satisfy Searle's theoretical requirements.

Indeed, much of what Searle says at this level in his fourth lecture is good, but the 'intentional causation' which he grafts onto it is wholly extraneous to the substance of what he says in that lecture. Thus he explains well how types of actions and behaviour cannot be identified with types of bodily movements (p. 57), how actions have 'preferred descriptions' which the agent himself is 'in a special position' to give (p. 58), and how these descriptions are 'constitutive' of the actions in question (p. 59). Though he does not discuss it, he is right to stress that the relation between an intention and the action which fulfils it is 'internal' (p. 60). However, when he brings in the notion of 'intentional causation' he goes wrong: 'Normally my desire will cause the very event that it represents . . . The cause both represents and brings about the effect' (p. 61).

What is 'represented' in my intention is not an event, it is an action. I do not bring that about, cause it to happen; what I bring about is an event. When I do so, my action is my bringing about that event. There is no sense in which my intention to do something causes that action to happen. Take the case of promising. Here I commit myself for the future. When the time in question comes I may say, 'I would like to go out with you but I can't. I have promised to see my brother.' This doesn't mean that I am forced to do what I previously promised, that my past promise causes me to do what I do. If that were the case I would be a bystander to my actions. To hold that is to take an epi-phenomenalist view of the matter, or at any rate a view that comes close to it (see p. 133 below). Indeed, I do not see how Searle can escape epiphenomenalism even with his two levels of description:

A. brain activity $\xrightarrow{\text{causes}}$ muscular contraction

identity $\parallel$

B. intention (a $\xrightarrow[\text{intentionally'}]{\text{'causes}}$ my arm to go up (lo and behold!)
macro-
property of
the brain)

Where do I fit, as an intentional agent, into this scheme? Do I 'initiate' my brain activity? Is this something I intend or cause? And if I initiate it, is that intention or cause another brain activity? If it is, then we are involved in a vicious regress. If it is not, then we have the case of an intention which remains unexplained on Searle's theory, an intention which floats with no physical anchorage. Either case spells disaster for Searle. His 'intentional causation' is a theoretical nicety which does not solve his problem. It seems that after all, if Searle is to remain true to his materialism, he must embrace some form of epi-phenomenalism and stomach the downgrading of the mind in status.

What Searle needs to consider is the way actions are originally constitutive of the intentions they embody, the sense in which (in Wittgenstein's words) an intention cannot be allowed to stop any-where short of the action intended (1963, sec. 615). He needs to be clear about what is wrong in thinking of an intention as a 'mental state'. In short, he needs to get clear about the difference between our common-sense view of these matters (as he calls it) and the Cartesian account, and see what is wrong with the latter. He is far from having done so; even in his positive account of human action he has not been able to shake off the Cartesian framework which dominates his whole discussion of the relation between the mind and the body.

When Searle speaks of the way 'the mind brings about the very state of affairs that it has been thinking about' (p. 61), he needs reminding that the mind neither brings about nor thinks about anything. This is no mere quibble. It lies at the source of Searle's puzzle. It is the flesh-and-blood person who brings about things by means of his actions, which are not themselves among the things which he brings about. *He* is the seat of causality; not a dis-embodied mind, however much Searle may think of it as 'rooted in' the brain in the very special sense which he explains. It is again this same flesh-and-blood person who thinks about things — things he can describe, handle and act on. What we have here, therefore, is not an instance of something 'weightless' representing some-thing tangible. If it appears so to Searle — and that is why he has to identify the mind with the brain — that is because of the Cartesian presuppositions which shape his thinking.

6. The mind – body problem

Does the body not act on the mind then, and the mind act on the body? Is there no causal interaction between the two? The short answer to this is no, not in the sense that 'there is no causal inter-action between them', but in the sense that thinking of the mind and body as thus divorced, even if only then to be identified — 'not two different things but one' — is all wrong. The idea that the mind and the body do interact causally presupposes the Cartesian divorce and starts us reflecting from the wrong base.

This is not to say that there is no mind – body problem. There is not one problem, but a whole host of interrelated ones. What we need to get clear about is *not* the relation between a Cartesian mind and a Cartesian body, but between what comes under 'mind' and 'body' in their *ordinary* sense — between our thoughts and actions, our thoughts and what we say, our emotions and their expressions, our capacity to perceive things and our capacity to identify and describe them, our perceptions of things and our reactions to them, our body, our limbs and organs of perception as we think of these in the first person and our physiology as we know this through our 'inductive experience' or books on physiology. There is a whole array of problems, an inquiry into which would involve making explicit and criticising, insidious presuppositions which bedevil our thinking when we think about these matters — that is, when we theorise and philosophise.

A simple solution to a mind – body problem such as Searle offers in his 1984 Reith Lectures is thus a philosophical mirage. Searle's lectures are indeed a very curious mixture of archaic metaphysics and modern, sophisticated philosophical ideas, some good and some bad. And his whole enterprise, the lectures, leave me with a sense of wonder at the wasted inventiveness of this very intelligent man, the wasted inventiveness which philosophy so very often is.

Notes

1. Dilman, 'Descartes and the Interaction between Mind and Body', in *Love and Human Separateness* (Blackwell 1986).
2. Not the ordinary sense of 'introspection', but a confused sense we come across in books of philosophy and psychology.

12
Thinking and the Brain

1. A critique of Cartesian interactionism

In a book entitled *Mental Abnormality: Facts and Theories*, Millais Cuplin writes:

> As a trained medical man I know that we live and have our being through physiological processes; that the brain is a wonderful and complicated organ, derangement of which can directly affect thought and emotion and action, that besides the brain there are other parts of the nervous machine that help govern our responses to the outside world.

Indeed, most people, including myself, would accept that derangement of the brain can directly affect thought, emotion and action. But when Cuplin speaks of the brain and the rest of the nervous system 'governing' our responses, the word 'govern' raises questions that need to be answered: Is he making anything more than the *negative* claim that if this or that goes wrong with this or that part of the brain then we are *unable* to do the things that we normally do, that various of our capacities are *impaired*? Or is he saying that somehow the brain runs our thinking in the way that a car's engine runs the dynamo? If he is saying the latter then he is making what is at least prima facie a highly paradoxical claim. Cuplin continues:

> Over and above all this [the brain and the nervous system] is the man himself, who thinks and feels and acts. His thinking, feeling, and action are functions of something we call mind.

What mind is we do not know, but we cannot carry on life without it, nor can we discuss our doings without taking it into account. Every process of the mind must have a counterpart in some process in the brain, but we do not know what the relationship is between the two.

He finishes the passage by describing the brain as 'the instrument of the mind'. So now it seems that his claim is that it is 'the mind that runs the brain' and not the other way around. From a materialistic position — 'we live and have our being through physiological processes' — Cuplin seems to have slipped into a dualistic one.

'Over and above all this is the man himself . . . His thinking, feeling and action are functions of something we call mind.' It is true that in one reading of it this is unobjectionable. It says that thinking, feeling and action are ascribable to the individual person. It is the man who thinks and not his brain; to think is to exercise a *mental* capacity, in this case an intellectual one. Put in this way the mystery ('what mind is we do not know') vanishes; thinking is the exercise of a mental capacity, that capacity belongs to the individual person, and it is he who exercises it.

However, Cuplin puts it differently and is perplexed: There is the brain with various electrochemical processes going on in it when we think, and there is the mind ('something we call the mind') with mental processes going on in it, which processes are our thoughts. The two go on in harness: 'every process of the mind must have a counterpart in some process in the brain'. But how are they related? It cannot be that the brain runs our thinking (though 'the nervous machine helps to govern our responses to the outside world') since it is each one of us ('the man himself') who 'initiates' his own thoughts. The brain is 'the instrument of the mind' and not vice versa. There is still an ambiguity here: Is it 'the man himself' who uses his brain as an instrument or is the brain 'the instrument of the mind'? Perhaps for Cuplin 'the man himself' is not the flesh-and-blood human being I took him to be. Perhaps, like Descartes, he identifies the man with the mind, thinking of the mind and the body in separation from each other, as if their identities were logically distinct.

So it is 'the man himself' who 'initiates' his own thoughts, who uses his brain to think. I shall try to come clean with my philosophical innuendos. Somewhat impatient, Cuplin may respond: Surely we do use our brains to think. We think with our brains.

This is, surely, common knowledge, marked by various expressions in our everyday speech. This knowledge has now been put on a sure medical footing by those working in the field — physiologists, anatomists, brain surgeons.

Of course, I agree that there is an intimate relation between thinking and the brain. The question is: What does it amount to? How is it to be properly conceived? These are philosophical questions and generally they act as magnets to confusion.

'We use our brains to think, we think with our brains.' The idea is that there is an analogy with the way we use computers to solve various problems, to search for answers to certain questions: 'What we used to do with our brains we now do with greater efficiency with computers. The computer has come to take over the function of the brain; it does the same thing, only better and more quickly.' We operate the computer, press various keys or buttons. Certain circuits are established as a result inside the computer. Then we get various visual phenomena on a screen; these constitute answers, in intelligible symbolism or language. The electronic connections made in the computer have no meaning in themselves and are one thing. But they 'determine' or 'govern' the intelligible messages on the screen. They are another thing, and in quite a different medium or logical dimension. What takes place inside the computer corresponds to our brain processes. What we see and read on the screen corresponds to our thoughts, our mental processes.

But this supposed analogy is defective in several respects. First, the person who uses a computer in the way described has to be taught and so learns how to operate the computer — what each key stands for, what buttons to press when he wants this or that, and so on. In contrast, we do not learn to operate our brains and, indeed, we know very little about our brains. In fact, we do not operate our brains at all. 'Use your brain' is only a metaphor. Indeed, our brain is not an instrument, and it is even more confusing to think of it as such than to think of our limbs and sense organs as instruments. For at least we manipulate objects with our hands, pick up a stone, turn over the pages of a book, we follow an object of sight with our eyes. Of course, we do not in turn manipulate our limbs and eyes as we manipulate instruments, a lever or a pair of binoculars. But, my point is, at least we move them at will, and in that sense they enter into our actions: I slap someone's face, I give someone else a nod of approval with my eyes. But my brain does not in that way figure among the objects of my intentions; it does not enter into my thoughts when I think.

111

We learn to use our hands, for instance, in performing some very delicate task. But we do not, in any comparable way, learn to use our brains to think. Indeed, we learn to think as we learn to speak — I mean 'acquire the capacity to think' — and we learn to exercise this capacity in various circumstances as we learn about the various things we learn to think about. We learn to think, speak and act in harness.

'Use your brain' is simply another way of saying 'think'; it says no more and no less. If I may put it like this: when we think, our brain is simply 'ticking over', and that is not something we do, whereas thinking is. Having found out that when I think the electrical activity in my brain increases, I could bring about such an increase by thinking about something, no matter what, as I might increase the rate of my pulse by running up and down the road. But, I repeat, this is not something I do directly; it is a consequence of what I do, something I bring about. Thinking, on the other hand, is not something I bring about or 'initiate'.

The activity of the brain enters into thinking in a way similar to the one in which nerve processes enter into perception and voluntary movements. Thus an excess of alcohol, for instance, will act on the central nervous system and prevent one from thinking clearly, as it will also slow one's reflexes. But it would be misleading to describe this by saying that the brain governs one's thinking.

Secondly, in the case of the computer, we see and read the symbols on the screen or the printout on the paper. We have caused these to come on by operating the keyboard. But we do not read our own thoughts, nor do we bring them about. We think them, and that means we think *about* something — the garden shed, for instance, that is no longer able to keep the rain out: we wonder, perhaps, what to do about it. Furthermore, we do not think about this *by means* of anything. Indeed, the content of my thoughts are the things I think about, and my thoughts are not something over and above these. Thus if you want me to tell you what my thoughts are, I would have to tell you what I have been thinking about.

Thirdly, in the case of the computer and the screen it *seems* (and I stress the 'seems') that mechanical processes determine or govern intellectual or intelligible ones. But this is a muddle. The screen, or the computer as a whole, does not 'tell' one anything or 'think anything out'. One presses certain keys and, given the intricate circuits inside the computer and the programme one has put in it, the machine goes through certain steps or stages, certain lights flash on and off on the screen, or a certain printout emerges. These have the shape of symbols, for that is how the thing has been designed. The fact that the lights have these shapes is no accident. The computer and screen were designed for certain uses, and it is *we* who use the computer as an instrument, as we may use a slide rule, and read what comes on the scrren. The symbols have no significance for the computer, and they are produced purely mechanically.

If we say that the computer is calculating, this is not different from saying that the excavator is digging. It is serving *our* purpose, the purpose it was built to serve. It cannot have one of its own. Wittgenstein once imagined a computer to have been washed ashore on a desert island and in good working order. The people on the island who found it started pulling its knobs out, whereupon the computer started working, producing sheets of mathematical symbols. In those circumstances could it be said that the computer was calculating?[1] The example is meant to illustrate that it is *we*, human beings who have certain purposes by virtue of belonging to a complex culture, who use the computer. What we describe it as doing is relative to those purposes. Shorn from that whole setting what the machine does cannot have the significance which our description of what it does attributes to it. It collapses to a series of mechanical movements. Similarly, the printout that comes out of it is just a series of black marks.

So what we have here is a series of mechanical or electronic causes, one kind of process — what goes on inside the computer. These determine another kind of electronic process — the lights that go on and off, making patterns on the screen. Just as when we use a slide rule, lining up certain numbered lines against one another, other numbered lines are lined up which one can then read off. This is a *result* determined by our move of the slide rule, given the way it has been constructed. We *use* this result, for instance, in an engineering project. It is in the possibility of such uses that its *significance* lies. It is like consulting logarithm tables. In separation from the human practices in which such results are used, the result obtained, the lights on the screen, have no significance whatsoever. The slide rule isn't thinking or telling us anything; it is an ingenious device, constructed by us, for making certain mathematical connections simply and quickly, which otherwise would take time and a number of complicated steps to make. (It has been designed, of course, in accordance with a sophisticated mathematical theory, that of logarithms.)

The connections on the slide rule are purely physical or spatial. These acquire a *mathematical* significance for us in what we make of them, the way we use the slide rule, the activities in which our operations with the slide rule enter. This is equally true of the computer.

It is not our brain which thinks, any more than it is the computer or the slide rule that calculates. It is *we*, human beings, who think, creatures who carry on a complicated mode of life, act and interact with each other. Leave all this out, and no matter how much the brain ticks over or the larynx and mouth move and emit certain sounds, we would not and could not have *thinking*, or speaking.

Not, however, because something else would be missing, namely the *mental* processes which *are* the thinking. This is the Cartesian idea of thinking as a process going on in a different realm from the physical, namely the mental or psychic. Thinking is not a process, something that goes on, in whatever medium, something that we initiate, by doing something else, pressing a button, physical or mental. It is not, for instance, an association of ideas, a string of mental images following each other in accordance with some law or other. *That* would be a process.

If I carry out a calculation, work out a particular problem, figure out the consequences of taking certain steps, or try to imagine what the sitting room would look like if I moved the furniture around a certain way, these would be examples of thinking, one kind of thinking which may be called reflecting, cogitating, reasoning. We could describe an instance of it as something *going on*, though one could also describe it as something *I am engaged in*. What is going on can be described as a 'process' only in the sense that it can be divided into a series of sequential steps. Beyond this to speak of it as a process — a mental process, a process in the mind — is misleading. For, as Wittgenstein has repeatedly pointed out, what is going on in such a case is a calculation only in certain surroundings. The reams of marks that come out of the computer on the desert island, to return to Wittgenstein's example, are not sequences in any calculation. Nor are the sequences that I may write down or recite, those that I may have learned parrotwise, unless I know mathematics and live a life in which they have some application. Whereas, in contrast, physical, chemical and biological processes take place in nature (erosion, the oxidisation of metals, the growth of fungi) regardless of what might or might not come before or after and surround them. Let me repeat: the sequences or steps add up to a calculation only, as Wittgenstein would say, in the application a living being makes of it, and that brings in the kind of life in which there is room for such applications.

Hence what goes on in the brain has as little relevance to the possibility of thinking as what goes on in a computer — the biological processes in the one case and the mechanical or electronic processes in the other. The most one could say — and that is what I would say — is that the processes in the brain, and everything that combines to bring them about, are *causally necessary* to thinking. I mean this in the sense that anything that would interfere with them would hinder the person in his thinking, or at least in his ability to think clearly; it might, for instance, confuse his thoughts. Certainly thinking does not go on in the brain, and whatever goes on in the brain cannot be what we call thinking. In that sense thinking does not go on anywhere, though I can think my thoughts in my head, verbally out loud, or on paper. In each of these cases what goes on is not thinking independently of the surroundings which my life gives it. You cannot, as it were, skim off what goes on from its surroundings and expect it to retain its identity as thinking.

The idea of thinking as a process is a persistent idea. Until one sees what is wrong with it one will be inclined to think either that thinking is a process in the brain or that it is something that goes on within one, in the mind. In the second case, one may think of it as an association of ideas or a train of mental images. Such innocent expressions as 'use your brain' and 'a penny for your thoughts' may then be misunderstood and compound the confusion. But once one recognises the sense in which the idea of a process gives us the wrong grammatical model for what thinking amounts to, one will also recognise that thinking need not be something that goes on 'within me'. Take one of the examples I mentioned earlier. I think first, if I move the settee to this side, it will make the room shorter. If I move it there, the room will look unwelcoming, and also the settee will then be too far from the fire. As for the chairs . . . and so on. First this, then that, then that, etc., and this may lead towards a resolution: this is the best way, or this is how I would like to have it. If anything is *going on* here it is precisely what I have described. Insofar as *that* is thinking, then thinking is what this example portrays as 'going on'. It is not something else that goes on *behind* what I have described, something going on *in* me. Here, while it is *I* who am thinking, the thinking that I do does not take place within me. It takes place outside me, open to public scrutiny, accessible to the participation of my wife who has also got tired of the arrangement of the furniture in our sitting room.

One can speak of 'the process of calculation' and of its 'result'. The process consists of steps, each of which we can scrutinise. We can ask whether it is correct. But we do not answer each such question by calculation. If I answer some questions by reflection, by working or thinking anything out, then there must be some questions which I answer without thinking anything out. This does not mean that I have answered them 'without thought' in the sense that the answer is simply the first thing that came into my head. I had my mind on the question, and I am someone who has learned and, therefore, knows the mathematics in question. I am, consequently, ready to stand by my answer. It is responsible to mathematical criteria and I take responsibility for its correctness; I am ready to support or justify it, to give reasons for it.

When I utter words without thought, what distinguishes what I say from the case in which I utter them with thought is not what does or does not go on within me. If that were the case people other than me could never be sure whether or not I had spoken them with thought. Nor could anyone be sure that the parrot does not think when he utters various phrases. Surely the difference lies in how I go on with the words I utter. If you were in any doubt you would question me about what I said, about the subject matter of our conversation, *not* about whether or not something went on within me.

So the difference between thoughtful and thoughtless words does not lie in the presence or absence of something going on within the person speaking them. Such a process is a philosophical fiction. Nor does the identity between what goes on in the different cases in which I am said to be thinking about the same thing — moving the furniture around in one case, gesturing towards the different parts of the room and uttering words in another case, drawing diagrams in a third case, sitting still and looking at the furniture with concentration in a fourth case — is a process going on within me, behind what I have described in each case, the same in all these cases. What makes these different descriptions of what I do in each case descriptions of the same thing, namely, thinking how best to arrange the furniture in the room, are the surrounding circumstances, the background, the before and the after. And the thoughts that are the same in these different cases are *in* the movements, *in* the gestures, *in* the words, *in* the diagrams.

In each case I am thinking how best to rearrange the furniture and what I have described myself as doing constitutes the thinking in question. Yet none would do so in itself. It is partly this that makes us think that the thinking must be something else, another process going on behind 'these coarser phenomena'. But this does not follow. For even though none of these things in themselves constitute the thinking in question, they do so in the particular circumstances of the case.

The following parallel may help to make the point clearer. Speaking, someone might say, is the uttering of words in grammatical constructions. That is not correct, since if a parrot did that, he would not be speaking. And someone who did that in a foreign language in the course of an exercise would not be speaking. But even if we were to grant this, someone may still ask what the words uttered in such constructions are: Are they sounds? If one says that they are sounds that have meanings, then this raises the question: What are meanings? What is it for a sound to be a word by having a meaning? Wittgenstein pointed out that we shall make no progress by considering what goes on in the minds of the speakers of the language. We have to consider instead what it is for a word to belong to language, and what it is for a people to have a language. We take all this for granted — the conditions that must be fulfilled for a people to have a language and for a person to be speaking it — when we say that someone has uttered a word or words and that he was saying something. It is only within such circumstances that the sounds he utters constitute speech. However much you arrange for the right sequence of sounds to come from a robot in the right circumstances you cannot make it talk. This is equally true of thinking. Furthermore, the circumstances that have to obtain are the same: thinking and speaking are interwoven and, as Wittgenstein said, we learn to think as we learn to speak.

It is within the circumstances of human life that what a person does constitutes thinking. It is not the stuff, the elements, nor simply their sequence that we need to consider, but the circumstances. In that sense, there is no one set of events or processes, 'inner or outer', that need to go on for a person to be thinking. Thinking is not something that can be identified with any process, physical or psychic — say a sequence of words or mental images — apart from special circumstances.

If we say that 'thinking is something mental' this does not mean that it is a process that goes on in the mind in the sense of being a sequence of mental events. If we speak of it as something 'mental', we are referring neither to a special medium in which it goes on, nor to any special stuff which constitutes it. We mean that it is the exercise of a *mental capacity*, mental as opposed to physical, in the sense of belonging to the body. What is in question is an intellectual capacity, not one that involves the muscles, for instance. But what has this capacity is the *person*, not something in him called 'the mind'. While this capacity is mental in this ordinary, common-or-garden sense, its exercise can take different forms. Thus I can think on paper just as well as, and perhaps in some cases better than, I can think in my head.

Cuplin, from whose book I quoted, says, 'His thinking, [etc.] are functions of something we call the mind.' This is a typically opaque philosophical statement. What might Cuplin be trying to say? We say, for instance, that his studies have developed his mind. This is not like saying that the exercises have developed his muscles. If you think that what is said is that his studies have developed something in him we call the mind, you will be misled. What is this thing called the mind? All that the above sentence means and says is that as a result of his studies, he can now think more clearly about matters related to the subject of his studies, reason more coherently, make better judgements. In other words he, this person, can now do certain things better than before, things which constitute the exercise of certain mental capacities. 'His mind' here is meant to refer to his capacity for judgement and reasoning. We are not talking of a special, ethereal substance within which certain processes go on.

Having said this, let us return to the question of how the body, including the brain, and the mind are related when a person thinks. We certainly can no longer think of this as the relation between two parallel processes taking place in the mind and the brain. Thus if the person is thinking with pen and paper, then the body is involved in the movements he makes, and these are an expression of the person's thoughts — I mean the marks and perhaps the gestures he makes. His thoughts are in what he writes, the writing itself being in a language he understands. As for the brain and its functioning, this constitutes the physical, bodily background necessary to thinking, much in the way that the optical nerve and its proper functioning is necessary to seeing, and nerves and muscles are necessary to voluntary movements.

Someone may say, 'Our memories are stored in our brains.' All that this means is that if a surgeon were to cut off certain parts of the brain one would no longer be able to remember what one is now able to remember. It isn't as if we scan certain parts of our brains when we try to remember, as when trying to find a document in our files. If you say, 'Yes, of course, we do no such thing, but all the same this is what happens in the brain,' then I ask, 'What is it that happens?' 'Electrical charges flow along certain circuits, and so the circuits must be there.' I reply, 'All right, so all this is necessary to memory, to remembering.' I go back to my earlier remark that when we think, when we remember, the brain, with its complex structures, is just ticking over. This 'ticking over', which can be investigated by physiologists, anatomists and brain surgeons, is causally necessary to the thinking. The particular structures in my brain make it possible for me to think certain thoughts, to remember certain things, in the sense that if they are removed or altered I can no longer think these thoughts, I lose the memories. This is as far as I would go.

It is still *I* who thinks the thoughts, remember — a person who acts, who interacts with other people, who lives the kind of life we live with language. In separation from all this, the brain structures in question could not make me think or act, as the circuitry and programme in a computer enable a robot to do various things which help us, say, in the construction of motor cars. Of course, what the robot does is to move in certain complicated but precise ways. It does not construct a motor car in the sense in which the people who run the factory do, and they use robots in accomplishing this task.

2. Searle's critique of strong artificial intelligence

I criticised one traditional way of understanding the relation between the mind and the brain, namely the Cartesian account of the way the brain is involved in thinking. Searle, in his second and third Reith Lectures, criticises two modern accounts of this relation — what he calls 'strong and weak artificial intelligence', the latter also called 'cognitivism'. He is right in rejecting both these accounts. However, in philosophy, it is not so much conclusions that count, even when they are negative, as how one reaches them.

Searle's second lecture is entitled 'Can Computers Think?'. The view that he is combating is that computers can think and that the brain itself is an organic computer. On this view the mind is related to the brain as the programme of a computer is related to the hardware: 'the brain is just a digital computer and the mind is just a computer programme' (p. 28). This is one modern form of materialism which downgrades the status of the mind, and Searle opposes it.

The gist of his refutation is that a computer, in contrast with human beings, performs the operations which it was designed to carry out without understanding. A computer may 'behave as if it understood', as if it had the understanding which human beings have in the operations they perform, such as when they work out the answer to a mathematical problem, but this is not enough.

While I would wholeheartedly go along with this, the question is: What is it that is not enough? What is it that is lacking in the case of computers? What is it, in contrast, that human beings have? In other words, what is it to have understanding? It is the way Searle spells this out which I find abstract, programmatic and unhelpful, and at times positively misleading.

> It is essential to our conception of a digital computer that its operations can be specified purely formally . . . A typical computer 'rule' will determine when a machine is in a certain state and it has a certain symbol on its tape, then it will perform a certain operation such as erasing the symbol or printing another symbol and then enter another state such as moving the tape one square to the left. But the symbols have no meaning; they have no semantic content; they are not about anything. They have to be specified purely in terms of their formal or syntactical structure . . .
>
> But this feature of programmes . . . is fatal to the view that mental processes and programme processes are identical . . . There is more to having a mind than having formal or syntactical processes. Our internal mental states, by definition, have certain sorts of contents . . . If my thoughts occur to me in strings of symbols, there must be more to the thought than the abstract strings, because strings by themselves can't have any meaning. If my thoughts are to be *about* anything, then the strings must have a *meaning* which makes the thoughts about these things. In a word, the mind has more than a syntax, it has semantics. The reason that no computer programme can ever be a mind is simply that a computer programme is only syntactical, and minds are more than syntactical. Minds are

semantical, . . . they have more than a formal structure, they have a content. (pp. 30–1)

I will not comment on the English of this passage, which is not irrelevant to its philosophy.

Searle then goes on to illustrate his point with what he calls a 'thought experiment' about a computer which simulates the understanding of Chinese. It uses its data base to 'answer' Chinese questions in Chinese symbols. He supposes that the computer's 'answers' are as good as those of a native Chinese speaker and asks: Does this mean that 'it literally understands Chinese'? Searle argues that it does not mean this, by comparing it with a person who does not speak Chinese and who is locked in a room with baskets of Chinese symbols and a rule book in English for manipulating these symbols, specifying the manipulations purely formally. To cut a long story short, a person can, in this way, be made to 'answer' Chinese questions in Chinese symbols without knowing what he is doing — that is, without understanding the questions put to him or the symbols he manipulates, and without knowing that the symbols he pushes out constitute answers to questions. In other words, while questions are put and answered, they are not being answered by the person in the room. He may not know the answer to the questions if they were put to him in English. He only does something which, unknown to him, has been arranged to have this consequence, namely that questions in Chinese are answered.

I agree with all this. Whatever he is doing cannot be described as 'answering the questions put to him in Chinese' since he does not speak or understand Chinese. What one needs to discuss here is what it is for a person to be a language speaker and what it is for him not to speak a particular language. The latter has not learned to respond spontaneously to people who speak to him in that language. I would not refer to 'internal mental states' or to what does or does not 'go on in his mind', nor whether what goes on has 'content in addition to syntactical structure'. Doing so does little to further the discussion or clarify what needs clarification; it may actually turn our attention in the wrong direction. As for the computer, the divide between it and the person who has not learned to speak a particular language is more radical than this. In the first part of this book I have criticised behaviourism. But I would still refer to the person's responses and behaviour and to the circumstances that surround them, those of a human life in which he participates. This is the direction in which I would move in articulating the differences between a human being and a computer.

Searle writes, 'Understanding a language, or indeed, having mental states at all, involves more than just having a bunch of formal symbols. It involves having an interpretation, or a meaning attached to those symbols' (p. 33). But again the question is: What is it for a sign or mark to be a symbol? What is it for it to have a meaning? What is it for me to attach a meaning to it, to know this meaning or understand it? These questions are not to be answered by looking within and considering what goes on in the mind, but rather by turning one's attention outwards and considering the life and behaviour of human beings. This is not to return to behaviourism.

Searle summarises his argument and conclusions as follows:

1. Brains cause minds.
2. Syntax is not sufficient for semantics.
3. Computer programmes are entirely defined by their formal, or syntactical structure.
4. Minds have mental contents; specifically, they have semantic contents.

Conclusion:

1. No computer programme by itself is sufficient to give a system a mind. Programmes, in short, are not minds, and they are not by themselves sufficient for having minds.
2. The way that brain functions cause minds cannot be solely in virtue of running a computer programme.
3. Anthing else that caused minds would have to have causal powers at least equivalent to those of the brain.
4. For the artefact that we might build which had mental states equivalent to human mental states, the implementation of a computer programme would not by itself be sufficient. Rather the artefact would have to have powers equivalent to the powers of the human brain. (pp. 39–41)

I have already discussed premiss 1, namely the idea that 'brains cause minds'. In separation from a human being, his life and responses, no matter what may be going on in the brain, we do not have a subject to which we can intelligibly attribute thoughts, feelings, perceptions, desires or intentions. The idea of 'brains causing minds' is a piece of sophisticated nonsense.

'Syntax is not sufficient for semantics.' If this is meant to refer to strings of symbols, then what it means is that the purely formal structure of the string is not enough. It must have a use, and that brings in the circumstances of human life. For it is only here that any string of words or symbols can have a use.

It is true that 'computer programmes are entirely defined by their formal, or syntactical structure'. But could this have been otherwise?

'Minds have mental . . . semantic contents.' What could this mean other than that human beings make sense of things? They do not simply interact causally with their environment. They respond to what has sense to them; it is this sense or significance that determines their response, given the way they feel towards it, rather than any causal properties of the things to which they respond. They have the ability to think about these things and about themselves, to form intentions and make decisions with regard to them. They can also make mistakes about the sense of things and reappraise this sense. Such a mistake is not like a breakdown in a mechanism.

If I understand them correctly, then I would go along with what premises 2 to 4 are trying to say in a jargon that is of little value, if not positively misleading. But then the crux of the problem is to get clear about the difference between the performance of computers on the one hand and human action and thinking on the other.

I agree with Searle's conclusion (in my words) that the fact that a computer has a programme doesn't entail that 'it has a mind' — in other words, that it is capable of thought and feeling, perception and intention. But this is not a matter of what is or is not sufficient to 'cause mind'. I can make no sense of that expression, and Searle's conclusion that brains have some special causal power which computers lack is the wrong way to look at the matter. What is in question has nothing to do with the causal powers of the brain. Those powers, whatever they are, may be necessary to a person's ability to think in the way I have explained earlier; but that does not mean that the thinking is a 'causal consequence' of their exercise.

Searle regards these causal powers as 'biological'. I do not see that this means that the substance that has them cannot be synthesised by man. When Searle says that 'mental states are biological phenomena' (p. 41) — presumably he means such things as thinking, feeling, and wanting — what he forgets is how much more important is the fact that they are social phenomena. If they are the result of generations of evolution, then man's social life and language are the most important products of this evolution.

3. Searle's critique of cognitivism

Searle begins his third lecture by pointing out that although we explain human behaviour well enough by referring to the agent's beliefs, wishes, emotions and intentions, 'we suppose that there must be a neurophysiological sort of explanation of people's behaviour in terms of processes in their brains'. But we do not know how to relate the first kind of explanation to the second. Yet we feel we ought to be able to do so since only the second kind of explanation is scientific. In other words, it is our scientific view of the world which leads us to require this. He writes:

> Some of the greatest intellectual efforts of the twentieth century have been attempts to fill this gap, to get a science of human behaviour which was not just commonsense grand-mother psychology, but was not scientific neurophysiology either. Up to the present time, without exception, the gap-filling efforts have been failures. Behaviourism was the most spectacular failure . . . I am going to claim that all the gap-filling efforts fail because there isn't any gap to fill. (p. 42)

'There isn't any gap between the brain and the mind.' This is Searle's thesis, that while the mind and the body interact they do not interact as 'two different things', since 'mental phenomena just are features of the brain'.

Those who have not had the benefit of Searl's philosophical enlightenment have attempted to fill this supposed gap. Searle points out that 'the most recent gap-filling efforts rely on analogies between human beings and digital computers. On the most extreme version of this view . . . the brain is a digital computer and the mind is just a computer programme' (pp. 42–3). The refutation of this view was the topic of Searle's previous lecture. Now he turns to cognitivism. This view too finds a strong analogy between the mind and computer programmes: 'it sees the computer as the right picture of the mind', but it does not claim 'that computers literally have thoughts and feelings' (p. 43). That was the 'strong artificial intelligence' view rejected by Searle.

Cognitivism characterises the brain 'at the level of its functioning as an information-processing system. And that's where the gap gets filled' (ibid.). In other words, the difference between the two views is this: one characterises the brain as a computer at the level of its structure, the other does so at the level of its functioning. It claims that when we think, for instance, the brain works *like* a computer and that between the brain's physiology and human 'performance' there is 'a level of mental processes which are computational processes' (p. 43).

Searle goes on to examine and criticise the arguments in favour of cognitivism. He mentions several, but the main ones he discusses are the following: (1) 'The formal rules of grammar which people follow when they speak a language are like the formal rules which a computer follows' (p. 45). This, Searle points out, derives from Chomsky's work. (2) 'Mental achievements must have theoretical causes.' In other words, 'if the output of a system is *meaningful* . . . then there must be some theory, internalised somehow in our brains, which underlies this ability' — for example, our ability to learn a language or to recognise faces (p. 45).

Searle writes, 'I don't believe that I have a knockdown refutation of cognitivism' (p. 46). But, even if this is true, his rejection of these two arguments in favour of it is, to my mind, conclusive. With regard to the argument from rules, he points out, quite rightly, that actually following a rule and going through steps which as a matter of fact, and not as a matter of intention, accord with a rule are not at all the same thing. This is a question which Wittgenstein discussed at great length, especially in his work on the philosophy of mathematics. He went into the differences between what he called 'causal determination' and 'determination by a rule'. When, however, Searle talks of 'meanings causing behaviour' and the 'semantic content' of a rule 'playing some kind of causal role in the production of what I actually do' (p. 46) he, like Kripke (1982), falls into the very misconception which Wittgenstein was combating, namely the idea that meaning and understanding are mental processes which determine the behaviour in which they find expression.[2] Criticising this idea, Wittgenstein points out that what a person does in following a rule is not the *result* of his understanding, but a *criterion* of it (1963, sec. 146). Indeed, I think that this idea is to be found in Searle's conception of 'mental' or 'intentional causation', which I have criticised earlier.

Still I completely agree with Searle's conclusion here:

In the sense in which human beings follow rules (and incidentally human beings follow rules a whole lot less than cognitivists claim they do), *in that sense computers don't follow rules at all. They only act in accord with certain formal procedures.* The programme of the computer determines the various steps that the machinery will go through; it determines how one state will be transformed into a subsequent state. And we can speak *metaphorically* as if this were a matter of following rules. But in the *literal* sense in which human beings follow rules computers do not follow rules, they only act as if they were following rules. (p. 47)

Searle then goes on to argue that just as a computer does not in a literal sense follow rules, similarly it does not do information-processing in any literal sense (p. 48). 'In the sense in which we have to go through information-processing, they [calculators] don't' (p. 49). As with rule-following, Searle goes on to distinguish between 'two senses of the notion of information-processing — or, at least, two radically different kinds of information-processing' (ibid.).

He calls the first 'psychological information-processing'. In the second, he says, it is only *as if* information-processing was going on. But again his characterisation of the difference is muddled by the confusions of his philosophical bias. The first, he says, 'involves mental states', whereas in the second 'there are no mental states'. Earlier he had said that the computer doesn't understand what it is doing; now he says that it has no mental states. Even if we were to grant that this is true, how is it supposed to clarify or explain the difference that is being studied? Here, if I may put it provocatively, what Searle needs is a dose of behaviourism.

He writes, 'when people perform mental operations, they actually think, and thinking characteristically involves processing information of one kind or another' (p. 49). All right, so when I am doing a long division mentally I am performing a mental operation. That is, I reach the answer by performing an operation in my head which involves the utilisation of my mathematical knowledge or skills. I say to myself, '5 goes into 26 5 times, remainder 1, etc.' But I do not reach the result at each step involved in the computation, itself by computation. If I may put it in Wittgenstein's style, my computations soon give out or come to an end, and I proceed without computation (see Wittgenstein, 1963, sec. 211).

Searle agrees. He considers a computer designed to help us identify faces or, may I add, thumbprints. It carries out 'quite a computational task, involving a lot of calculating of geometrical and topographical features' (p. 52). This 'involves complex information-processing' of the 'as if' variety. But it doesn't follow (he points out) that *we* recognise or identify faces in the same way, that is by any form of computation. He then generalises: 'For a great many absolutely fundamental abilities, such as our ability to see or our ability to learn a language, there may not be any thoeretical mental level underlying those abilities' (p. 53). This is right and important, and it is Searle's answer to the argument that 'mental achievements must have theoretical causes' (p. 45), that 'behind all meaningful behaviour there must be some internal theory' (p. 51). It is worth pointing out that Searle's argument (p. 52) is purely *a priori*, and it is the same as the one Norman Malcolm uses against Köhler's idea that a 'sussessive comparison' is impossible unless it rests on a 'simultaneous comparison'.[3] Cognitivism takes this idea further and holds that 'simultaneous comparison of unanalyzed wholes' must rest on 'simultaneous comparisons of analyzed structures'.

So far so good. Searle continues: 'the brain just does them' (p. 53). He thus brings the description to a physiological level: 'We are neurophysiologically so constructed that the assault of photons on our photoreceptor cells enables us to see' (p. 53). If by 'enables' Searle means 'makes it possible for us to see', in the sense that were we otherwise constructed, or were this structure interfered with or prevented from functioning, we would not be able to see, then I would pick no quarrel with him. But Searle makes a stronger claim; he means that these processes 'cause' seeing: 'Think of our visual experience, for example, as the end product of a series of events that begins with the assault of photons and ends somewhere in the brain' (p. 54). I have already criticised this part of Searle's view earlier.[4] It is nonsense, as I have pointed out, to say that 'the brain just does them' — sees, thinks, etc. It is *we*, individual people, who have these abilities, some primitive and some acquired through learning, and *we* exercise them in the course of a life we share with others. This is not a matter of what our brain does. As I put it earlier, our brain just ticks over.

'It's an obvious fact that the brain has a level of real psychological information processes . . . thinking goes on in their [people's] brains . . . What is psychologically relevant about the brain is the fact that it contains psychological processes and that it has a neurophysiology that causes and realizes these processes' (p. 50). This is the kind of nonsense that would be plain but for the fact that it forms part of the consequences of a sophisticated philosophical theory for which Searle has put forward highly intricate arguments.

Searle finishes this lecture by summarising his conclusions. First he has criticised the arguments in favour of cognitivism and the assumptions behind these arguments. Second, he says, he has shown that 'we do not actually have sufficient empirical evidence for supposing that these assumptions are true' (p. 55). Third, he has presented:

> an alternative view . . . of the relationship between the brain and the mind; a view that does not require us to postulate any intermediate level of algorithmic computational processes mediating between the neurophysiology of the brain and the intentionality of the mind . . . In addition to a level of mental states, such as beliefs and desires, and a level of neurophysiology, there is no other level, no gap filler is needed between the mind and the brain, because there is no gap to fill. (p. 55)

I think that Searle has selected some important arguments and criticised them successfully. But I do not see that the assumptions in question are empirical in character and so could have or fail to have evidence supporting them. Thirdly, Searle would not need to argue for a position in which 'no gap filler is needed between the mind and the brain' if he had been able to get Cartesian dualism out of his system. We do not need a philosophical theory such as Searle's or any other, in order to understand the role which the brain and the nervous system play in human thinking and behaviour. What we need is philosophical discussion which would include both criticism of philosophical presuppositions and clarification of familiar concepts and their relations.

At the beginning of his third lecture Searle said, '[W]e suppose that there must also be a neurophysiological sort of explanation of people's behaviour in terms of processes in their brains.' But why must there be? Indeed, how could there be? There are, of course, explanations of how the central nervous system functions, and knowledge about how breakdowns in this functioning affects human thinking and behaviour. But that doesn't mean to say that normal human behaviour can be explained in terms of neurophysiology. The supposition in question comes from certain misunderstandings. Most of Searle's problems to which, after many arguments, he finds a general 'solution' stem from his inability to reject this supposition.

Notes

1. Reported by Rush Rhees during a seminar.

2. See Dilman, 'S. A. Kripke, *Wittgenstein on Rules and Private Language*', *Philosophical Investigations*, October 1985.

3. See Malcolm, *Thought and Knowledge*, p. 152. Köhler gives expression to this idea in his book, *The Place of Value in a World of Facts* (New York, 1938), pp. 269–72.

4. See also Dilman, *Love and Human Separateness*, Ch. 1, 'Descartes and the Interaction between Mind and Body', section 5, 'Perception and Bodily Processes'.

13

Freedom and Determinism

1. Searle's antinomy

At the end of his last lecture, entitled 'Freedom of the Will', Searle restates the general aim of his lectures: 'to try to characterize the relationships between the conception we have of ourselves as rational, free, conscious, mindful agents with a conception we have of the world as consisting of mindless, meaningless, physical particles' (p. 99).[1] Searle calls the first our common-sense conception of ourselves. There is much that is sound in his spelling out of this conception. He goes wrong, however, as I tried to bring out, where he tries to relate it to the scientific, *materialistic* conception of the world, and, in particular, when he speaks of the relation between the mind and the body. Then he relapses to a Cartesian view of the mind as when, for instance, he speaks of an intention to raise my arm as a mental event which causes the physical event (p. 93).

Seeing that science has modified what was our common-sense conception of the world, Searle points out, we may understandably be tempted to think that it can similarly modify our conception of ourselves and of our behaviour. We saw that Skinner thought so and tried to bring this about. Searle, in contrast, points out that science cannot in this way radically modify our everyday conception of ourselves. I think that he is absolutely right. But if so, he reasons, in being unable to depart from our everyday conception of ourselves, are we not stuck in a position that is inconsistent with our scientific view of the world? He believes, as we have seen, that this is not so: 'My general theme has been that . . . our common-sense, mentalistic conception of ourselves is perfectly consistent with our conception of nature as a physical system' (p. 99).

I have argued that there is no inconsistency between the conception which the scientist — physicist, chemist or biologist — takes of what he is studying and our everyday conception of ourselves, and so no need for any reconciliation. Such a need arises only if one turns the scientist's conception of the things and phenomena he studies into a metaphysical conception of reality — materialism. Because Searle does so, he has a problem on his hands. His solution is a philosophical theory which I have characterised as a 'materialistic dualism' — a dualism fitted into the framework of a materialistic conception of the world. Thus Searle believes himself to have been successful in his task of reconciling the two conceptions: the mind has those features which our common-sense conception of ourselves attributes to it, namely 'consciousness', 'intentionality', 'subjectivity' and 'causal efficacy', yet at the same time it is caused by the brain and is, indeed, an aspect of the brain — its features are properties of the brain.

In our common-sense conception, Searle points out, we also think of ourselves as 'free agents'. But how can *that* be reconciled with the scientific, *deterministic* conception of the world or universe?

> Ideally, I would like to be able to keep both my common sense conceptions and my scientific beliefs. In the case of the relation between mind and body, for example, I was able to do that. But when it comes to the question of freedom and determinism, I am . . . unable to reconcile the two. (p. 86)

In my discussion earlier (see p. 107) of Searle's notion of 'mental causation', I pointed out that Searle cannot escape epi-phenomenalism even with his two levels of description: Do I 'initiate' my brain activity? If so, is my causality in doing so itself a brain activity? If it is, we are involved in a vicious regress, and if not, then we have an intention which remains unexplained on Searle's theory. This is what comes home to Searle in his last lecture:

> Since all the surface features of the world are entirely caused by and realized in the system of micro-elements, the behaviour of micro-elements is sufficient to determine everything that happens. Such a 'bottom-up' picture of the world allows for top-down causation (our minds, for example, can affect our bodies). But top-down causation only works because the

top level is already caused by and realized in the bottom levels. (p. 94)

Obviously, this view leaves 'no room for the freedom of the will' (p. 93). To make room for it, Searle says

we would have to postulate that inside each of us was a self that was capable of interfering with the causal order of nature . . . We would [that is] have to contain some entity that was capable of making molecules swerve from their paths. (p. 92)

But Searle very much doubts that 'such a view is even intelligible' (ibid). Consequently he is in a fix. He doesn't see that our common-sense view of ourselves as free intentional agents can be intelligibly abandoned. Yet it seems to him that the successes of science have incontrovertibly established the validity of a materialistic, deterministic conception of the world. And these pull him in opposite directions.

In this way, Searle is close to Kant in the formulation of his third antinomy. For Kant too rejected Hume's compatibilism and found causality and freedom irreconcilable. However, Kant found a solution to his problem in his 'transcendental idealism': causality is confined to the 'phenomenal world', whereas human freedom pertains to the 'noumenal world'. We are capable of free action because our 'noumenal self' is not subject to causality; the will is capable of 'autonomy' because we can detach ourselves from and so transcend our phenomenal selves, which are subject to the causality of inclination.[2]

But this way is not open to Searle. He speaks of the mind as being 'a part of nature', that is, as belonging to what Kant described as the phenomenal world, and he rejects any conception of reality that is not logically continuous with the field of science. So he believes that 'the problem is likely to stay with us' (p. 86).

2. Why Searle's problem admits of no solution

Searle presents the case for the freedom of the will forcefully. If I understand him rightly, this case rests on the untouchableness of our conception of ourselves as conscious beings capable of thought and intentional action. The possibility of free action is bound up with our being such agents. I entirely agree with Searle, though no doubt this connection can be spelled out in much greater detail.[3]

But if we really have freedom of will and action, Searle thinks, and quite rightly, then our actions must orginate in us. We must be their author and not be merely a link in a chain of causes that pass through us. His conception of the relation between the mind and the body, however, does not permit this. For though the mind is active and there is such a thing as 'mental causation', the mental processes which cause our actions are themselves caused by what happens in the brain. As he puts it:

> Our basic explanatory mechanisms in physics work from the bottom up. That is to say, we explain the behaviour of surface features of a phenomenon such as the transparency of glass or the liquidity of water, in terms of the behaviour of micro-particles such as molecules. *And the relation of the mind to the brain is an example of such a relation.* (p. 93)

It is precisely what is said in this last sentence, which I have italicised, that needs rejecting. It makes a far-reaching philosophical assumption in favour of which there is little to say, if anything at all. All right, on Searle's view 'mental processes' are *not* epi-phenomena since they have causal efficacy. But this is hardly an advance on epi-phenomenalism, since they are still little more than reflections of what takes place in the brain. If they are to be more than this so that our free will is a reality, Searle reasons, then there must be something in us which initiates or controls what takes place in the brain; there must be 'some mental energy of human freedom that can move molecules in directions that they were not otherwise going to move' (p. 87), 'a self inside each of us capable of interfering with the causal order of nature' (p. 92).

Searle finds such an idea unintelligible. Why? Someone may say: But we do interfere with the causal order of nature all the time. We build dams to harness the energy of water, we deflect the course of rivers, we build balloons which rise up into the air despite the force of gravity. However, we use our knowledge of causality and the laws of nature, we initiate and employ causal processes to do so, and it is the only sense in which we can oppose or alter 'the course of nature' which is governed by causal laws. Given, then, that this is not what the possibility of 'radical freedom' requires, what is it that it does require? The answer is that we should have the ability to make molecules swerve from their paths *by magic*. And it is indeed difficult to give an intelligible content to this idea.

As Wittgenstein put it in the *Tractatus*: 'what the law of causality is meant to exclude cannot even be described' (6.362). One has only to contrast 'the law of causality' which says that 'every event must have a cause' or 'nothing happens in nature without a cause' with a causal hypothesis, however general, which if true could be false, to see the reason for what Wittgenstein claims.

Elsewhere I contrasted the so-called law of causality with the hypothesis that smoking causes lung cancer. Let me quote two paragraphs from what I said:

> What does it [the law of causality] exclude? For instance, that lung cancer may have no cause? What does that mean? Of course, nobody may know for sure *what* causes lung cancer, and there was presumably a time when faced with such a disease scientists had no idea where to begin their investigation and what to investigate. Presumably, as they studied particular cases, compared and contrasted them, developed criteria of identification and so began to form a particular conception of the disease, ideas of how its causes are to be investigated began to emerge. Such a development, presumably, took place side by side with many other similar developments in other areas of human knowledge and within the very broad framework of a general pattern — the pattern of causal inquiry.
>
> That a particular disease, such as lung cancer, may not have a cause is now unthinkable. That lung cancer may have no cause is not an hypothesis open to investigation. For what would an investigation be here but a causal one! Our very notion of disease . . . brings in the idea of a causal investigation, so that particular diseases . . . raise causal questions for us. And a causal investigation is undertaken to find out *what* are the causes of a particular phenomenon; *not* to find out *whether* such phenomena have a cause. As Rhees once put it: ' "Some things happen without a cause" is shocking when it is said in connection with causal inquiry, because it seems to be a statement in the grammar of causal investigation.' (Dilman, 1984, pp. 151–2)

To return. If the will is free then our willing must itself not be subject to any cause. Now this sounds at once both right and absurd. It *is* right if it claims that if the will is free it must not be determined by anything external to it. One kind of instance in which it is so determined is the case of posthypnotic action. What such a person does is not what he has chosen to do, for what he does is scripted, and he cannot depart from the script. He cannot do so because he doesn't know that he is obeying orders and in that sense following a script. A philosophical sceptic may ask: Could it not be that everything I do is just like this? For if it were I would not know that it was so and think of what I do as I think of it now. And if it were true of me, could it not be true of everyone else as well? Could it not be that all human actions are caused in this way by a malevolent Cartesian demon who has hypnotised us for all time? In such a case we would have the consciousness of freedom, as at present, without possessing a will that is free in reality. That is, our consciousness of freedom would be illusory and we would have no means of finding out that this was so. This is a species of the argument from illusion used to bring into doubt our perceptual knowledge, and it can be 'refuted' in the same way (see Dilman, 1984c). Searle agrees that all human behaviour cannot be like that of 'the man operating under post-hyponotic suggestion' (p. 90). However, he thinks that what the sceptic suggests is just 'very unlikely' (p. 91), whereas I am saying that one can argue that it cannot be given any intelligible content. But let that pass.

So it is not impossible for the will not to be 'psychologically' determined by something external to it — for example, by hypnotic suggestion. But Searle holds that it is impossible for it not to be physically determined by causes that operate on the molecular level: 'the mind can only affect nature insofar as it is a part of nature. But if so, then like the rest of nature, its features are determined at the basic micro-levels of physics' (p. 93).

What does Searle mean when he says that 'the mind is a part of nature'? People sometimes say that '*human beings* are part of nature'. I understand this. It is a reminder for which there is a point on certain occasions: 'men do not live by their reason and intellect alone, they have appetites and instincts — they have a kinship to other animals'. If, however, in this sense *we* are 'a part of nature', it should not be forgotten that we also have powers or capacities which set us apart from nature, indeed which enable us on certain occasions to overcome those inclinations in us which make us 'a part of nature'. Unlike animals we can speak, think, form intentions, are conscious of and can reflect on our own inclinations and motives, and endorse or repudiate them. We act with knowledge of what we are about and have conceptions of good and evil which make a difference to what we do.

None of this, however, is what interests Searle when he says that 'the mind is a part of nature'. This is a metaphysical claim which *seems* to support Searle's 'materialism', but in reality it is only an expression of it. To put it boldly, it is 'false'. Willing and intending are embedded in a nexus of reasons which have their roots in the person. They are responsible to the person's beliefs and desires, to his appraisals and feelings. Certainly they do not come out of the blue, as the notion of 'radical freedom' requires. But that is not to say that they are effects of causes that are external to the person. Indeed, causality in the sense that concerns Searle does not come into this at all. My claim can be justified by an examination of the discourse in question, its concepts and its logic. That causality, in the sense that troubles Searle, must come into it is a philosophical requirement and prejudice.

Earlier I quoted Rhees: ' "Some things happen without causes" is shocking *when it is said in connection with causal inquiry*, because it seems to be a statement in the grammar of causal investigation.' Acting, willing, intending, deciding do *not* fall within the sphere of any causal investigation such as those we find in physics and chemistry. I do not mean that these things 'have no causes', but that it doesn't make sense to speak of their causes in the scientific sense. Nor, as I argued earlier, does it make sense to speak of them as causes themselves — 'mental causes'. That whole way of speaking belongs with Cartesian dualiasm, in which view they are conceived as 'mental states' or 'mental processes'.

We can, of course, ask, 'What caused you to do such a thing?' But this question is not answered in the way that questions such as 'What caused the twitching of his mouth as he was speaking?', and 'What caused the bomb to go off?' are answered. The answer may be: 'It was my anger that made me do it.' But the relation of my anger to my action is not an 'external' relation such as the one between a spark and the explosion it causes. And I have a way of answering this question which no one else can have without being me.

So my will is not a 'gratuitous spontaneity' or 'some mental energy' that can deflect molecules from their causally or statistically determined courses. But that does not mean that it is the effect of causes external to it. What Searle calls 'radical freedom' (pp. 92, 98) does not exist; it is a confused notion. But that isn't to say that free will is an illusion and that men can never act freely. If those alternatives seem to exhaust the field, it is Searle's philosophical assumptions that are responsible for this. The 'solution' of

Searle's antinomy, therefore, would turn on their criticism and rejection. I have indicated what I think is wrong with them.

Notes

1. Searle is not using the terms 'mindful' and 'meaningless' in their normal, everyday sense. Thus it is only a human being who can be said to be 'mindful' or 'mindless'. Such sloppiness in his use of language runs throughout his lectures, and I don't believe that it is without philosophical consequences.

2. For a discussion of one aspect of this see my paper, 'Reason, Passion and the Will', *Philosophy*, April 1984.

3. Stuart Hampshire and Jean-Paul Sartre are two philosophers who have done so. Thus see the former's *Thought and Action* and the latter's *L'Etre et le Néant*.

Bibliography

Cuplin, Millais, *Mental Abnormality: Facts and Theories*.

Day, Willard, 1977. 'On the Behavioural Analysis of Self-deception and Self-development' in *The Self: Psychological and Philosophical Issues*, ed. Theodore Mischel (Blackwell).

Descartes, René, 1927. *Selections*, ed. Ralph M. Eaton (Charles Scribner).

Dilman, İlham, 1975. *Matter and Mind, Two Essays in Epistemology* (Macmillan).

—— 1984a. *Frued and the Mind* (Blackwell).

—— 1984b. 'Reason, Passion and the Will' in *Philosophy*.

—— 1984c. 'Philosophy and Scepticism' in *Philosophy and Life, Essays on John Wisdom*, ed. İlham Dilman (Martinus Nijhoff).

—— 1985. 'S. A. Kripke, *Wittgenstein on Rules and Private Language*', in *Philosophical Investigations*.

—— 1987. *Love and Human Separateness* (Blackwell).

Dostoyevsky, Fyodor, 1957. 'The Grand Inquisitor' in *The Brothers Karamazov*, vol. i, trans. Constance Garnett (Everyman's Library).

Drury, M. O'C., 1973. *The Danger of Words* (Routledge and Kegan Paul).

Hampshire, Stuart, 1959. *Thought and Action* (Chatto and Windus).

—— 1961. 'Feeling and Expression', Inaugural Lecture at University College, London (H. K. Lewis and Co.).

Hull, C. L., 1943. *Principles of Behaviour* (Appleton-Century).

Hume, David, 1967. *A Treatise on Human Nature*, ed. L. A. Selby-Bigge (Oxford Univeristy Press).

James, William, 1948. *Psychology*, abridged edition (The World Publishing Co.).

Katz, David, 1979. *Gestalt Psychology* (Greenwood Press).

Köhler, Wolfgang, 1929. *Gestalt Psychology* (Horace Liveright).

—— 1938. *The Place of Value in a World of Facts* (Liveright Publishing Co.).

Kripke, Saul, 1982. *Wittgenstein on Rules and Private Language* (Blackwell).

Linden, Eugene, 1981. *Apes, Men, and Language* (Penguin).

Malcolm, Norman, 1964. 'Behaviourism as a Philosophy of Psychology' in *Behaviourism and Phenomenology*, ed. T. W. Wann

(University of Chicago Press). Also in 1977, *Thought and Knowledge* (Cornell University Press).

—— 1977. 'Wittgenstein on the Nature of Mind', *Thought and Knowledge* (Cornell University Press).

Mill, John Stuart, 1948. 'Utilitarianism' in *Utilitarianism, Liberty, and Representative Government* (Everyman's Library).

Miller, George A., 1979. *Psychology, The Science of Mental Life* (Penguin).

Mischel, Walter and Harriet, 1977. 'Self-control and the Self' in *The Self: Psychological and Philosophical Issues*, ed. Theodore Mischel (Blackwell).

Plato, 1973. *Gorgias*, translated from Greek by W. Hamilton (Penguin).

Rhees, Rush, 1969. 'Religion and Language', *Without Answers* (Routledge and Kegan Paul).

Russell, Bertrand, 1949. *The Analysis of Mind* (Allen and Unwin).

Sartre, Jean-Paul, 1943. *L'Etre et le Néant* (Gallimard).

Searle, John, 1984. *Minds, Brains and Science*, The 1984 Reith Lectures (B.B.C. Publication).

Secord, Paul, 1977. 'Making Oneself Behave: A Critique of the Behavioural Paradigm and an Alternative Conceptualisation' in *The Self: Psychological and Philosphical Issues*, ed. Theodore Mischel (Blackwell).

Shotter, John, 1975. *Images of Man in Psychological Research* (Methuen Paperback)

Skinner, B. F., 1947. 'Experimental Psychology' in *Current Trends in Psychology*, ed. Wayne Dennis (The University of Pittsburgh Press).

—— 1953. *Science and Human Behaviour* (Free Press Paperback, The Macmillan Co.).

—— 1964. 'Behaviourism at Fifty' in *Behaviourism and Phenomenology*, ed. T. W. Wann (The Univeristy of Chicago Press).

—— 1973. 'Answer to my Critics' in *Beyond the Punitive Society*, ed. Harvey Wheeler (Wildwood House).

—— 1976. *Walden Two* (Macmillan Publishing Co.).

—— 1979. *Beyond Freedom and Dignity* (Penguin).

Taylor, Charles, 1977. 'What is Human Agency?' in *The Self: Psychological and Philosphical Issues*, ed. Theodore Mischel (Blackwell).

Weil, Simone, 1950. *La Connaissance Surnaturelle* (Galimard).

Winch, Peter, 1958. *The Idea of a Social Science* (Routledge and Kegan Paul).

Wisdom, John, 1952. *Other Minds* (Blackwell).

Wittgenstein, Ludwig, 1961. *Tractatus Logico-Philosophicus*, trans. David Pears and B. M. McGuinness (Routledge and Kegan Paul).

—— 1963. *Philosophical Investigations* (Blackwell).

—— 1964. *Philosophical Remarks* (Blackwell).

—— 1967. *Zettel* (Blackwell).

Index